IGNES FATUI

Charles Thomas Taylor

University Press of America,® Inc.
Lanham · Boulder · New York · Toronto · Plymouth, UK

Copyright © 2012 by
University Press of America,® Inc.
4501 Forbes Boulevard
Suite 200
Lanham, Maryland 20706
UPA Acquisitions Department (301) 459-3366

10 Thornbury Road
Plymouth PL6 7PP
United Kingdom

British Library Cataloging in Publication Information Available

Library of Congress Control Number: 2012948513
ISBN: 978-0-7618-6013-6 (paperback : alk. paper)
eISBN: 978-0-7618-6014-3

TABLE OF CONTENTS

PREFACE (In the Form of a Parable)

And it came about that when the time of Zeus had become as that of the time of Cronus, a coregency of Apollo and Dionysus was established to govern the affairs of the gods and of men. But while this arrangement served perfectly for the gods, it turned out otherwise for men. For whenever Apollo intoned his voice of reason, it was quickly silenced by the noises of revelry, of passion, and of chaos. For Dionysus quite easily usurped the sovereignty of Apollo and so became the sole regent of men throughout all of the ages.

Yet men considered and looked to the stars, and saw that the gods had never been happy with the services of Dionysus alone. And they reconsidered that they might do well to restore Apollo to his rightful place in the original coregency. But they saw also, among themselves at least, that Apollo could neither be the master nor the peer of Dionysus, but only the servant. And so it came to pass that Apollo was restored as coregent with Dionysus, and through his artful subordination to his brother, he ultimately gained ascendence in the affairs of men.

ACKNOWLEDGEMENTS

I wish to acknowledge my indebtedness to the genius of Francis Bacon, whose *The New Organon* has served as a precedent, inspiration, and point of departure for the current work. I wish also to acknowledge the influence of certain other giants in the course of intellectual history whose contributions may find some small reflection throughout the content of my book: most notably Aristotle, Hegel, Darwin, and Sartre.

Finally, I wish to acknowledge the incredible technical assistance and cheerful support of Marie Ajour (who has worked with me in many past projects) in preparing this manuscript for publication.

INTRODUCTION

In every age, human knowledge advances to a certain extent at various locations in the world so that our understanding of reality becomes somewhat better than what it had been in the past. Some of these advances in human knowledge involve contradictions or refutations of that which we previously had thought that we understood quite clearly while others merely develop and enlarge an initial rudimentary understanding. To the extent that our knowledge conforms with our experience and that it appears to hold up in the face of various periodic challenges, we can say that it appears to be valid, that we must have grasped the truth, that we have seen the light; to the extent that it does not, we must candidly admit that we have been laboring under the influence of erroneous premises, that we have failed to grasp the truth, that we have been deluded by false lights.

Since the Scientific Revolution of the seventeenth century and the Enlightenment of the eighteenth century, human knowledge has flourished in Western Europe, particularly within the areas of scientific technology and human psychosocial self-consciousness. One of the most striking consequences of this intellectual blossoming has been the ascendence of democracy in the political organization of nations. The process of national democratization continues at the present time and suggests an ultimate convergence of progressive political paths in a global federal union of national democracies.

Another of the monumental advances in human knowledge which have erupted in modern history has been the discovery of the evolution of life—including, of course, the evolution of the human species—through the work of Charles Darwin during the nineteenth century. The discovery has led to further developments in the fields of paleontology, genetics, and neurobiology. We have a better understanding of the human mind today as a consequence of new discoveries in these fields: how the human mind is comprised of a prototypical reptilian brain (itself comprising the basal ganglia, the thalamus, the hypothalamus, and the amygdala—all located in the lower section of the brain just above its union with the spinal column) which controls movement and instinctive behavior; how such is then fused to a paleomammalian brain which accommodates the limbic system and an extended amygdala and which controls those mental processes which can be associated with those of mammals at the time when they first appeared and began to evolve, particularly the sensibility of the family as the distinctive social structure in the life experience of an individual mammal; and how in turn this initial fusion is further fused with a neomammalian brain which accomodates the neocortex (or frontal cortex) and which controls that ability *to think* which distinguishes all of the more highly developed and more recently evolved mammalian orders and families, such as the elephants, the dolphins, the canines, and the primates (within which order, of course, man is classified as a distinct genus and species within the family Hominidae). Now, the thought processes of a man are largely conditioned by his experience as a social animal, which is to say, by the influences of his culture. On rare occasions or in rare individuals, a man's mental processes may not exceed those of a reptile, a bird, a rodent, or a monkey, but we are not concerned here with such uncommon and infrequent anomalies. That which we *are* concerned with is a man's *thought* processes and how that which he *thinks* is largely derived from his particular cultural experience and the current condition of general human knowledge within his culture. We can draw one conclusion from these observations: wherever certain elements of human knowledge within a culture can be found to be obsolete or faulty, the thinking of a typical member of any given society within such a culture will likewise be faulty or obsolete.

It is our purpose now to expose such faulty thought so as to facilitate the inevitable cultural integration and future progress of the entire human species. At once, our critique will involve objective and subjective elements. The latter will be involved as we regard a person primarily as a private entity, when we consider the thought processes of a person as such may concern his or her personal affairs. The former will be involved as we regard a person primarily as an element of a social entity, when we consider the thought processes of a person who is but a member of a group, such that that person's ideas and values are in close conformity with the norms and opinions maintained by the group—as such norms and opinions should or should not fully reflect the current condition of general human knowledge. Where it should not, the thinking of the people may contain much that is ambiguous or contradictory but even where it should, it is quite possible that the thinking may eventually be found to be faulty and obsolete. Our discussion will begin with a consideration of the more objective elements of human thought, and such will proceed according to the categories of the major ideologies of a typical society: religion, politics, and economics. Since ethics may be considered both as a component of religious society and of secular society (and since, in the case of the former, the ethics of religion may best be considered apart from the metaphysics of religion), we will discuss ethics in a separate section. As we proceed, we will clearly observe that many of the instances and patterns of faulty thinking persist as obsolescences from the remote past which we have been unable to discard with any appreciable degree of ease because of our obstinate and long-standing biological inheritance as mammals in possession of a deeply emotional nature.

I.   IN RELIGION

To begin, we would refer to the research of the English anthropologist, Edward B. Tylor, who posited that animism, "the general belief in spiritual beings," is the most primitive religion. He further posited that animism has been observed in every known primitive society of the world. From these facts, and because we can conclude that animism alone must be the most primitive of religions because of its simplicity and immediacy, we might further infer the possible presence of animism among the families and tribes of Paleolithic man even some 500,000 to 1,000,000 years in the past.

Next, let us establish the fundamental rational faculties of which the paleomammalian brain of Paleolithic man was capable of possessing. These must most certainly have included perceptive, emotive, volitive, and cognitive functions (since we can find the same today among the other higher primates) and among the cognitive functions we must further include memory, imagination, and inference.

Now, imagination and inference certainly have had a deep-seated and torturous reciprocity all the way through the long mental evolution of the human species. With Webster's dictionary as our guide, we may recall that imagination is "the art or power of forming a mental image of something not present to the senses or never before wholly perceived in reality" while inference is "the act of passing from one proposition, statement, or judgment considered as true to another whose truth is believed to follow from that of the former." Inference can furthermore be classified either as deduction (inferring from the universal to the particular) or as induction (inferring from the particular to the universal).

With the triumph of empiricism in epistemology during modern history, the marriage of imagination and inference is no longer troubling since our acquired knowledge can eventually be validated by experience. This fact allows us enormous freedom to engage in creative thought throughout all of the sciences for our mutual benefit as well as the self-actualization of our individual existences.

This marriage was very different for Paleolithic man. Let us consider as an example the phenomenon of sound. Paleolithic man observed that living beings create sound: a baby cries, a person shouts, a wild beast roars, an axe striking a rock makes a noise. Then when he perceived such sounds as the crackling of fire, the flowing of water in a stream, the howling of wind, and the clapping of thunder—meanwhile, looking about in the direction of the sounds and observing no living beings—he quickly inferred that the sounds were created by invisible living beings. It is then not too difficult to understand how the concept of the supernatural gradually arose in the minds of our early progenitors.

Paleolithic man observed that a particular person dies. All of the movements and vitality of the person cease. The liveliness of the person had always been there before but now it is no longer present. Where did it go? Perhaps it left the body forever, became invisible, and took up a new residence somewhere else.

Paleolithic man likewise observed that human families and tribes were organized according to a hierarchy of power with alpha males, beta males, alpha females, beta females, and then all of the rest, just as in the groups of various animals with which he may have already been familiar such as packs of wolves or troops of chimpanzees. Surely, then, he would have inferred that the societies of supernatural beings were organized in a very similar manner.

The emergence of a belief in gods and goddesses undoubtedly occurred much later at a time much closer to our own, a time no further back than about 10,000 years ago, when Neolithic man first settled into loosely organized fixed settlements for the purpose of growing plants to produce food and clothing. At about this time, or sometime thereafter, supernatural beings were imagined to enjoy a far more perfect existence than that of human beings and the supernatural realm was likewise imagined to be far removed from the natural world of human existence. At this time also the various mythologies of the isolated clusters of human communities undoubtedly began to germinate and to take root.

Let us now consider the presence of religion in modern life. There are several old and well-developed religions which are still active in the world today but the five predominant religions which have exerted the greatest influence and consequently have attracted or compelled the greatest number of adherents include Buddhism, Christianity, Hinduism, Islam, and Judaism. All of these emerged from the polytheism that was prevalent among the earliest civilizations five or six thousand years ago. All of them impose upon their adherents a certain way of looking at the world. The Eastern religions, Hinduism and Buddhism, are deeply pessimistic and each provides a well-developed and comprehensive system of ethics to cope with, and ultimately to transcend, a recurrent, painful, and sorrowful human existence. The Western religions, Judaism, Christianity, and Islam, are more decidedly monotheistic (although the realm of supernatural beings generally include other supernatural beings which are subordinate to the supreme being, of which number at least one is conceived of to be extremely dangerous and detrimental to the concerns and interests of human beings), and the relationship between human beings and the supreme being conditions the ethics which the adherents of these religions practice and propagate. The origin of monotheism likely occurred during the reign of Pharaoh Ikhnaton 3,350 years ago when he briefly abolished polytheism in ancient Egypt and established the sole supremacy of the sun god Aton. In *Moses and Monotheism*, Freud has even directly identified the origin of Judaism with this historic event. The earliest supreme beings were conceived of as omniscient and omnipotent, requiring of human beings their total obedience and the offering of regular ritualistic sacrifices. Upon further cultural development, the supernatural metaphysics of these religions became entwined with interpersonal ethics. Eventually, the harsh features of the supreme beings softened as they abruptly transformed into compassionate self-sacrificing heroes on behalf of humanity. This sociological phenomenon constitutes the pinnacle of religious development in world history up to the present moment. The characteristic features of compassionate benevolence and self-sacrificing altruism are most readily apparent today in mainstream Christianity and Mahayana Buddhism.

1. THE PROBLEMS ARISING FROM THE THEIST WELTANSCHAUUNGEN

The world today in the second decade of the 21st century is comprised of approximately seven billion people. If current demographic trends continue, scientists project that the population of the world will increase to nine billion people within a few more decades. Now, some of these people are religious and some are not. Most of those who are and some of those who are not have a distinct way of looking at the world. Let us henceforth refer to the various outlooks of the adherents of the three predominant Western religions as the theist weltanschauungen. Their common features may generally be described in the following terms: human existence in the world is painful and sorrowful because human beings have become alienated from the supreme being who created them; in the absence of a satisfactory communication and relationship with the supreme being, human beings are powerless to satisfy the needs or to avert the hurts of their existence through their own efforts; if human beings do believe in and do communicate with the supreme being in a unilateral, gracious, and respectful manner throughout their lifetimes, and if at the same time they do adhere to a prescribed code of ethics which defines and determines the relationships between human beings as well as the relationship between human beings and the supreme being, then upon their deaths human beings will be reunited with the supreme being to live forever in a world of continuous comfort and happiness. (With certain minor but necessary modifications, this fundamental outlook may also loosely be said to hold for the adherents of Brahmanic Hinduism and Mahayana Buddhism).

It is not too difficult to see with perfect clarity that a rational outlook is totally incompatible with the theist outlooks. Certain problems immediately arise. To begin, the existence of beings (let alone that of a supreme being) in a supernatural world cannot be proven. Neither can the continuation or the rebirth of human existence following death be proven. Yet the theist weltanschauungen, which experienced such a rich birth in the human imagination but which received such poor nourishment from human reason during the long morning of the species, persist because they have provided, and they continue to provide, a convenient and plausible ideological structure by which to address the problem of human existence. Belief in things which have never been proven and which never will be proven because they *cannot* be proven is a relatively small problem. The rejection and consequent unavailability of various other possibilities by which to address the problem of human existence—because such possibilities are precluded by the general belief in things which cannot be proven—creates the greater problem. In other words, religious people are generally ultraconservative and highly skeptical of new approaches for the solution of the problems of human existence. Unless they can be persuaded that a proposed rational plan of human cooperation is compatible with their religious outlook, they will withhold or subvert their support for such a plan. This problem explains in part why human cultural progress has been so slow throughout the past.

Furthermore, the ascendence of reason, of empiricism, of democracy, and of universal public education in modern history has created a crisis of religious faith that has led to the emergence of bad faith both in religious and in secular matters of human concern. In the language of Sartrean paradox, we may define bad faith as "not believing what one believes, and believing what one does not believe" and it has created enormous ambivalence, apathy, and irresolution in the mental outlook of many religious people today throughout much of the world. As a consequence, people who profess to be religious sometimes talk or act as though they were not, while people who do not profess to be religious sometimes talk or act as though they were. In either case, their words and their actions are halfhearted and ineffectual. The ubiquity of bad faith in modern life creates enormous, and often insurmountable, problems in interpersonal relationships as well as in efforts toward social cooperation.

Finally—and certainly this is the problem of greatest danger and concern, a problem which could not arise if the entire world adhered to a uniform religious faith with no division of opinion or interpretation, a problem which increasingly imperils the very survival of the species—the religious faith of any particular religion is at once self-righteous and intolerant of the religious faiths or the philosophical positions of outsiders, leading to universal divisiveness, the continual failure of cooperative efforts within the global human community, and the ultimate certainty of annihilative religious warfare. That this last issue has presently become a problem of such gravity as to imperil the very survival of mankind is a consequence not so much of its identity with the penultimate position in the outlook of certain Western religions (as evidenced by their eschatological scriptures) but of the rapid ascendence of scientific technology in modern history and the recent and very alarming proliferation of nuclear weapons throughout the world.

2. THE PROBLEMS WHICH CAN BE PREVENTED WITH THE SOCIETAL TRANSMUTATION PHASE OF THE HUMANIST WELTANSCHAUUNG

On the other hand, a small portion of mankind has formulated a more hopeful and rational alternative. A transition in human thought from a god-centered world to a human-centered world occurred independently at two specific locations within the Eurasian land mass, one in the East and one in the West, approximately 2,500 years ago. The power of religion in human culture was ubiquitous throughout the entire world at that time, but its force in ancient China and in ancient Greece was no longer as powerful as it had once been or as powerful as it could still be found to be in most other places, and some men there began to think about themselves and their place in the world with a free and courageous independence from the influence of the traditional religions. In both places the thinking became anthropocentric in the sense that it would lead to some new understanding that could provide significant value for human beings in their interactions among themselves and with their environment. The scope of such thinking evidently was much broader in ancient Greece than in ancient China, where it was primarily concerned with ethics. An example of an early self-awareness of this transition can be found in the Protagorean maxim "Man is the measure of all things" and we may be fully justified in acknowledging that humanism was born in ancient Greek philosophy.

The power of Christianity thrust humanism into a shadow for 1,500 years until its rediscovery during the Renaissance; since then, however, it has been developing with increasing vigor and clarity. The abiding characteristic feature of humanism is the steadfast conviction that the ultimate recourse for the solutions to the problems which confront human existence will be found in human reason alone. The ascendence of humanism over the past five hundred years has been accompanied by the ascendence of empiricism in epistemology, of Einstein's general theory of relativity in physics, of Darwin's theory of evolution and of Mendel's principles of heredity in biology, of democracy in politics, of regulated capitalism in economics, and innumerable other substantial advances in human knowledge. At the present time, sufficient progress has been achieved to enable us to formulate a general Humanist weltanschauung. Perhaps we might describe it in the following terms: human beings are a unique species of animal life living finite lives in a natural environment in which the power of hereditary instinct has gradually weakened while the capacity to employ the rational faculties of the mind has gradually strengthened as to allow the various members of the species to confront the problems of their existence with a combination of autonomous and collective thought and behavior; since the capacity to employ the rational faculties of the mind is far more advanced in human beings than among the members of the other species of animal life, and since the possession of reason is common to all members of the human species, human beings can be said to be more alike than different and it is in the general interest of all human beings that the universal should always be preferred and favored over the particular in all of such human affairs which affect everyone; while human beings are imperfect beings, and while in certain qualities they will always compare unfavorably with individuals of various other species, they can strive individually and collectively toward an optimality of human thought and behavior to attain personal happiness and societal well-being, and the ultimate object of such striving may be said to be the paradigm of human perfectibility.

We can now see with perfect clarity that such a broad outlook immediately suggests the inevitability of the formation and perpetuation of a universal society under a single federal democratic government, once all or most of the remaining oligarchies in the world shall have transformed into national democracies and once the remaining barriers of mistrust, ill will, and disdain have been eradicated between the various national democracies. Then two of the problems arising from the theist weltanschauungen to which we previously alluded will disappear. Firstly, the critical problem of the eventual certain self-destruction of the species through catastrophic religious warfare can easily be avoided as more and more people are converted from espousal of the various theist weltanschauungen to espousal of the Humanist weltanschauung. Secondly, the problem of the rejection by the adherents of religion of various possible plans which are likely to be formulated through rational thought and discussion for the effective solution of common human problems, and the problem of any consequential refusal to cooperate with those who might advance such plans, can be avoided as well. It is impossible to predict the length of time which must elapse before these benefits can be achieved but with recent accelerating advances in human knowledge and transnational communication, we must hope and resolve to act together decisively to make certain that a universal democratic society will quickly emerge before either the total destruction of the species or an irreversible general decline in human civilization.

3.   THE PROBLEMS STILL PERSISTING EVEN AS THE THEIST WELTANSCHAUUNGEN GRADUALLY CONVERGE TOWARD THE HUMANIST WELTANSCHAUUNG

Reason and religious faith, or religion and Humanism, are at once in the service of human emotions so that human beings may be able to attain and to maintain an optimal degree of happiness. Nonetheless, they are essentially incompatible and each has endured despite the continuous presence and influence of the other throughout human existence.

There is one small parcel of common ground upon which reason and religious faith stand together: namely, the shared concept of ethical heroism. By this we mean the concept of the individual who sacrifices his or her personal well-being, and possibly even life itself, while engaging in personal actions for achieving the survival or well-being of others. Aristotle referred to such "highmindedness" as "the crown of the virtues" (*The Nicomachean Ethics*, Book IV, Chapter VII). A pattern of cultural development culminating in the heroism of Achilles and Aeneas is readily apparent in the mythologies underlying the civilizations of ancient Greece and Rome. A similar pattern can be discerned in the development of religion, beginning with the animism of primitive societies, progressing to the polytheism of the earliest civilizations and the monism or monotheism of certain of the more recent civilizations, and culminating in both Christianity and Mahayana Buddhism with the heroism of a supernatural supreme being that sacrifices itself for the ultimate well-being of all of humanity. In Christianity, the concept of divine sacrifice has become anthropocentric with the concept of the holy trinity, and specifically through the concept of the person and role of Jesus, the Son of God. The model of Jesus' life is cast as a paradigm of human perfectibility in the Christian weltanschauung even as personal self-actualization by means of reason and personal effort, culminating as it must in ethical heroism whenever and wherever such personal initiative may be conceded as acutely necessary and absolutely unavoidable, may be taken as a paradigm of human perfectibility in the Humanist weltanschauung. Through this common ethical paradigm and to the extent that the metaphysical aspect of religion may be seen to be slowly losing its force during the ascendence of empiricism throughout the world, we can say that the theist weltanschauungen are gradually converging toward the Humanist weltanschauung.

In a democracy, unanimity is not necessary for the achievement of political action. It is only necessary for a specified majority to indicate their common consent to a proposed course of public action at any given time. So it is with the persistence of religious faith in human existence. There is and ever will be no limit to the absurdities in which some human beings will allow themselves to believe. The most that we may be able to expect at the beginning of the long afternoon of the species is that a majority of human beings will embrace a faith in humanity or in human reason alone and that, as a necessary consequence, they will totally and permanently reject religion in all of its forms. For those persons who will not, two problems will persist—one, the absurdity of believing in something which can never be proven and two, the continuing presence of bad faith in human affairs with consequential ambivalence, indecisiveness, and ennui, the degree of the cumulative magnitude of which will generally vary in direct proportion to the number of such persons. For this reason among many others, we will do well always to possess patience with other human beings, ever hopeful to persuade them of the error of their convictions through the supreme power of reason.

II.   IN ETHICS

Since we can infer that belief in the supernatural must have been an ubiquitous conceptualization throughout the later phases of the early evolution of the human species, we can also infer that religious ethics must have always served as a crucial factor in the cultural development of prehistoric man. Since that portion of religious ethics which concerns interpersonal relationships occurring in the natural world can often be found to have had some rational basis, and since the much later rise of critical rational thought approximately 2,500 years ago at diverse locations in the world very often included a distinctly ethical component, we can acknowledge that ethics has also been conceived, or otherwise at least confirmed, developed, and refined by means of rational thought, in total independence of its original conception and longtime presence in religious thought. A person may accept the tenets of a body of ethics which either has an essentially religious foundation or an essentially rational foundation. The motivation of such a person in accepting the former will be to avoid (upon the imagined onset of a life after death) the judgment of a wrathful god with the consequential condemnation to an existence of eternal punishment, and to enjoy instead the immediate presence of a loving god with the consequential gift of an existence of eternal comfort, pleasure, and happiness; the motivation in accepting the latter will be quite simply to enjoy a more secure, desirable, and happier existence until death. Now, there is much in the tenets of religious ethics that does not directly concern the well-being of human beings during the course of their lifetimes or their relationships with each another but instead encourages antiintellectual thinking and evokes useless ritualistic activity designed to placate imagined supernatural beings, an unfortunate combination of attitude and behavior that generally detracts from human efforts to meet the demands and to avert the hurts of life. For this reason alone, we can readily see that we would do better to reject an ethics conceived in religion and to accept one wholly conceived or validated in reason. A much stronger reason to reject the ethics of religion is to avoid the persistent problem of bad faith (and all of its detrimental effects) which arises in the enormous and continuous uncertainty surrounding the reality of the supernatural world.

When we *do* succeed in severing the ties which bind ethics to religion, we confront yet another problem. To envision this problem with some measure of clarity, let us refer to the hierarchy of needs model of Maslow's theory of human motivation. This model is sometimes graphically represented with the image of a pyramid. Let us imagine a pyramid with five tiers. The large base accommodates the physiological needs. The second and somewhat smaller tier accommodates the safety needs. The third (and still smaller) tier accommodates the love, affection, and belongingness needs. The fourth and next to the smallest tier accommodates the self-esteem and honor needs, and the apex accommodates the self-actualization need. Now, an effective ethical model is intended and constructed to secure the optimal well-being of society and its members, individually and collectively, even as an effective theory of human motivation is intended and constructed to secure the optimal well-being of the individual. When we attempt to integrate any one of the ethical systems which have been formulated through human reason with the hierarchy of needs model, we can readily observe that an objective ethics, that kind of rationally derived ethics that erects the necessary foundation for the entire legal system of a society (such as, for instance, the ethics that have been derived from the principles of non-injury and utility) is instrumental in satisfying the lower needs (the physiological needs and the safety needs). This kind of ethics, when appropriately adopted and applied, will always elevate us to approximately midway up the pyramid but never all the way to the apex. Our new problem is that we may accept our rationally derived ethics, an objective ethics evoking non-injury, justice, and useful activity, as a complete and comprehensive body of ethics when as such it is in fact incomplete and consequently inadequate. To accommodate the higher needs, we largely need in addition a subjective ethics, such as the ethics that have been derived from the principles of reciprocity and magnanimity. Now, by our use of the term "a subjective ethics," we do not wish to imply in any sense that whatever should be designated "subjective" is totally or even largely nonobjective: such would only be true in the case of any thinking occurring during the hallucinatory phase by a person inflicted with a severe mental illness such as schizophrenia or bipolar disorder. Rather, by a "subjective ethics," we simply mean that a person's adoption of such an ethics, whether in full or only in part, is discretionary, not obligatory (with the exception only of an obligation voluntarily assumed under an inferred interpersonal moral contract, a contract to provide personal assistance to other persons during a time of personal adversity when assistance to such persons is vital for their survival and is otherwise unavailable), and that a person may enjoy a considerable degree of freedom with respect to his or her interpretation and application of its fundamental tenets. When we include such an ethics alongside the totally objective ethics which we have previously discussed, we will be fully able to secure an equilibrium between the dichotomy of freedom and justice in society and consequently to secure the optimal well-being of society while at the same time preserving a secure and supportive environment in which each member of society can be free to attain, to sustain, and to intensify his or her unique self-actualization. Furthermore, a distinctly subjective component of any ethical system that has an essentially rational foundation will effectively supplant its counterparts among the various religious ethical systems so that those who may choose to abandon or to reject religion because of its irrational features will always still possess an easy and effectual access to the knowledge of optimal human behavior.

III.   IN POLITICS

From the outset, we have recognized the ascendence of democracy in the political organization of nations throughout modern history. This ascendence first occurred (with varying degrees of success in the initial implementation and subsequent refinement of democratic government) in Western Europe, the Americas, and Australia, and it later encompassed much of Central and Eastern Europe, Asia, and Africa. Although democracy has engendered isolated and distinct prototypes throughout ancient and medieval history, its relatively recent eruption and subsequent rapid ascendence is distinctly a modern political phenomenon. It has largely supplanted the earlier oligarchical forms of government which were prevalent among the various societies of the world since Neolithic times. Those oligarchies were the natural outgrowth of the form of family leadership that was prevalent among our prehistoric ancestors, in which an alpha male assumed the leadership position supported by a small cadre of subordinates: one or two beta males and sometimes an alpha female. The remaining members of the family, comprising a majority, assumed a specific but often fluid role within the group according to a descending rank of social status. Although this state of affairs has persisted for a very long time and although it obviously has a very powerful biological foundation in the species, the presence of oligarchy in modern times—when reason has flourished and human beings have finally attained some small but clearly discernable modicum of personal and social self-awareness—has merely delayed the attainment of an acceptable and functional level of personal freedom and social justice in most of the societies where it is still operable. The reason why oligarchy cannot endure is quite clear: whenever a minority imposes by force its will upon a majority, the consequential suppression and curtailment of personal freedom and social justice will eventually arouse resentment, discontent, and revolt among the majority. Accordingly, the only rational form of government for any society today (with the possible exception of the societies of primitive people which can still be found in remote locations of the world) is one in which all of the members participate, directly or indirectly and to the extent to which they may be able, in the decisions and actions of the society as a whole. For this reason, we must at long last firmly reject oligarchy and all of its various forms, both ancient and modern. Alternatively, we must enthusiastically accept, promote, and strive to improve democracy. Our greatest challenge, of course, is to analyze, to evaluate, and then to refute those governments today which *pose* as democracies in various stages of early development but which actually operate as disguised oligarchies, as when an elite group provides leadership for a society ostensibly on behalf of all of the citizens with their various interests but actually to secure and to perpetuate unjust privileges and advantages for the members of the ruling class. Besides such Trojan horses of democracy, which we obviously need to identify, to expose, and to overturn, there are certain political philosophies, interpretations of political concepts, and forms of government which are commonly associated with democracy today (as they have been for some time) but which are clearly irrational or otherwise essentially contradictory to democracy, and consequently they are inappropriate for the further development and refinement of democracy. We will now proceed to discuss these in turn.

1. THE PROBLEM OF THE CONSTITUTIONAL MONARCHY

Notwithstanding our characteristic possession and occasional employment of the faculty of reason, human beings are at worst but one more species of animal life and as such, we can neither easily avoid nor transcend our common biological heritage. Evolving as we have from the higher primates, our most typical political associations have long emerged as intense power struggles both within and between family groups. During those infrequent ages of enlightenment when conceptual social improvement and consequent cultural progress sometimes easily erupted, the conceptual superiority of democracy over oligarchy was often readily apparent (paradoxically) to a few gifted thinkers but by the time that the majority of the people had gradually come to be aware of the concept, the massive weight of human biological heritage—the power of tradition, the resistance to change, the glorification of the past, the fear of the future, the comfort taken in habitual and customary behaviors—precluded a permanent transition from oligarchy to democracy. Notwithstanding certain salient events and developments relevant to the gradual ascendence of democracy in the history of England and of Great Britain—the Magna Carta (1215), the Commonwealth of England (1649-1659), the Glorious Revolution (1688), Chartism (1838-1848), the founding of the Labour Party (1900), the Commonwealth of Nations (1949)—the British monarchy persists. In continental Europe, the French Revolution quickly gave way to the rise of Napoleon Bonaparte, who attempted to spread democratic reforms throughout Europe by means of French imperialism that was consciously modeled after the imperialism of ancient Rome. The obvious absurdity of such a contradiction subverted an opportunity for the immediate triumph of democracy and facilitated the perpetuation of the traditional oligarchies until the conclusion of the two world wars. The irrational (but otherwise very human) development of democracy in France, with the recurrent alternation of monarchy and republic, has yielded a ridiculous paradigm of democracy for other societies to emulate. Responding to the tumultuous momentum of modern world history, other monarchies in Europe, Asia, and Africa have adopted constitutions to justify the enduring coexistence (by means of hybridization) of an ancient feudalistic oligarchy with a modern parliamentary democracy, but the absurdity of the paradox is quite evident for everyone to recognize. Clearly, the continuing general progress of democracy, including the future course of national democratization of the remaining oligarchies of the world and world federalization of the existing democracies of the world, over and above the future course of personal and social optimization within any given democracy, will be best served when the remaining constitutional monarchies of the world, including the British monarchy, quickly transform themselves into democratic republics. The validity of this premise should be so self-evident that nothing more need now be argued on its behalf.

2. THE PROBLEM OF ANTI-INTELLECTUALISM

The ascendence of reason over the obstinate forces of human biological heredity in the modern history of human affairs presume a common devotion to the pursuit and acquisition of knowledge and truth. Indeed, the sudden birth, the lengthy anemic infancy and childhood, and the ultimately robust adolescence of democracy as the quintessential political offspring from the ascendence of reason has demanded a citizenry that must be literate, educated, and sufficiently trained to assess, to evaluate, and to judge competitive facts and opinions in the world of ideas. The ascendence of reason, and of democracy, suggests a love of reason, a devotion to truth, a desire for knowledge, a commitment to learning, and an aptitude for thinking.

The greatest danger for an emerging democracy arises when a large number of people are engaged in physical labor to obtain the basic necessities of life without the benefits of machinery and technology. This sociological phenomenon is often prevalent in rural areas of new democracies where antiquated agricultural methods are still followed, or in urban areas where primitive industrial methods are commonly practiced. The heavy burden of such work, which must often begin during childhood, precludes an adequate education for the citizens of the democracy and generally leads to the formation of a common attitude of anti-intellectualism.

An attitude of anti-intellectualism is fundamentally antithetical to the favorable development of a healthy democracy. When the population of a society holds a common attitude of anti-intellectualism, political decisions will be made that are primarily based upon irrational and emotional factors with the consequence that the democracy, at best, will be largely ineffective in meeting the needs and desires of its citizens and, at worst, will succumb to subversion and self-destruction, abruptly reverting to yet another version of ancient oligarchy. Indeed, this phenomenon is precisely what appeared in Germany with the emergence and subsequent ascendence of National Socialism upon the inauguration of the Weimar Republic at the end of World War One.

Even among democracies which have already experienced some measure of political continuity and favorable social development, the insidious danger of some recently formed common attitude of anti-intellectualism—arising as it may during a period of severe adversity consequent to a natural disaster or an economic downturn—may suddenly come to light. In this event, the accumulated experience of the citizenry will be tested in the effort to preserve the democracy.

In all events, reason will ultimately prevail, and democracy, if it should have died, will experience a subsequent rebirth, or if it may have survived, by some expediency or another, it will more thoroughly adapt itself to conditions anew and eventually begin to thrive.

The inadequacy of personal decisions, or of social policies, which are solely concerned with the immediate gratification of personal and collective appetites and emotions—decisions and policies formulated in the heat of passion and not in the light of reason—should have been clearly evident without the facticity of our having commented upon it. Conversely, to the extent that the members of a democratic society can retain their faith in reason, and remain faithful in the use of their rational faculties to seek solutions for their problems, whether such problems be those which they share in common or those which are unique to their private interests, their lives will be all the more secure, stable, and happy, and the well-being of their society all the more assured.

3. THE PROBLEM OF MERITOCRACY IN A REPRESENTATIVE DEMOCRACY

When democracy first erupted in ancient Athens approximately 2,500 years ago, its original form and content was necessarily restricted by its adaptation to the primitive conditions of Greek society at the time. The two most onerous conditions included, of course, (1), the institution of slavery and (2), the subordination of women to men (with the practical consequence that women were not permitted to participate in political affairs). Ancient Athenian democracy is generally characterized as a "direct democracy," meaning that an assembly of all of the adult males (excluding resident aliens and slaves), known as the *ecclesia*, would elect public officials and pass legislation. However, even in a society with a population as small as that of ancient Athens (relative to the populations of most modern democratic states), some consideration and employment of agency or representation quickly became necessary for the everyday practical administration of public affairs. Apparently, the Council of Five Hundred was instituted by Cleisthenes—comprised of 50 men chosen by lot each year from each of the ten tribes of ancient Attica—to deliberate relevant public policy and to prepare important political issues for discussion and election by the assembly. The representatives served in the council for one tenth of the year and were paid for their services from public funds.

Since human populations have increased substantially in the course of modern history as a consequence of dramatic advances in science and technology, modern democracies by necessity are of the indirect or representative kind (although very recent advances in communications technologies may eventually enable a favorable modification of this current cultural phenomenon). It may be important to recall that the mechanism for the selection of the system of political representation which was introduced by Cleisthenes was deliberately designed to depend upon chance because, in the absence of a direct participation in government by all of the citizens, any citizen among the electorate should have had an opportunity to be chosen for service as a representative of the electorate that was the equivalent of that that was available to any other citizen. Now, if it can be successfully argued that the overall quality of a democracy can never exceed the cumulative quality of the intelligence, education, awareness, interest, and concern of its citizens, then it may seem possible to argue that only those of the citizens who can demonstrate an above-average level of intelligence and education should be permitted to serve in the government as a representative of the people. Two counterarguments should suffice to refute such an argument. Firstly, a representative who has been selected on the basis of demonstrable merit because he or she has met or surpassed certain established objective minimum standards of intellectual and educational competence for public service may nonetheless have a level of awareness of, interest in, and concern for current public affairs that is distinctively inferior to that of a citizen who does not meet such standards but who would otherwise enthusiastically volunteer to serve as a representative. Secondly, even if a representative who has been selected on the basis of demonstrable merit as previously described should likewise demonstrate at least an acceptable—if not an exceptionally high—level of awareness, interest, and concern, he or she may not always necessarily meet the same standards during the course of the term of his or her service as a representative because of some failure during that time to sustain the personal initiative, enterprise, and discipline that had been present and instrumental during the course of one's education.

To conclude the present discussion, we would at once definitively argue against any future inauguration of a system of meritocracy in a representative democracy (for the reasons which we have previously cited) and possibly argue in favor of a reinstatement of the system of representation that was introduced by Cleisthenes long ago in ancient Athens (modified as it may be necessary for it to be adaptable to the conditions of a modern democratic society). Under such a system, citizens could be randomly selected for service of a limited term as representatives in the legislative and executive branches of government in a manner very similar to the present manner in which they are randomly selected for jury service. We believe that the Cleisthenes model of political representation in a democracy may be an idea worthy of substantial further development.

4. THE PROBLEM OF A PATERNALISTIC AND DISCRIMINATORY INTERPRETATION OF SOCIAL JUSTICE

Primates have evolved over the past 20 million years in such a manner that the family forms the fundamental social unit, and the structure of the family generally centers upon a single alpha male whose behavior, to a very large extent, directs and influences the social behaviors of the other members of the family, and to a lesser extent, the one-to-one relationships between the various members. The same biological phenomenon continued to hold when the early families of man coalesced into larger family groupings—extended families, clans, and tribes—and eventually into the temporary or permanent alliances between family groupings with common biological and linguistic heritages. The social dynamics of primate societies in their natural environment have emerged in such a manner that *power* has become the supreme individual and social value, with the apparent consequence that infants who are too weak or too sick to thrive are left to die, as are the young male members of the family who fail to learn the necessary skills to attain adequacy as hunters and fighters, notwithstanding the powerful biological instinct of the mothers in the group to nourish and to protect their own offspring and sometimes even the offspring of their closest female relatives. Since, in general, the stature and physical strength of females is not as great as that of males, the status of females in most of the societies of the great apes and of man has always been inferior to that of males, and newborn female infants are often neglected. Adult members of primate families, and particularly the oldest members who have lived well past their prime, are frequently abandoned to die, once they have succumbed to weakness and disability from sickness or injury. On the other hand, the stronger members of the group are permitted to perpetuate their strength: they receive the choicest items of food, they dominate and exploit the weaker members, and they control most of the breeding that takes place within the group.

In the course of the long development of human culture, these powerful primatial biological predispositions have continuously directed and influenced its progress until the beginnings of the systematic cultivation and employment of the mental faculty of reason which occurred infrequently at various isolated times and places concurrent with the ascendence of civilization over the past five thousand years. Even the concept of social justice has been so colored by our long human biological heritage and cultural traditions that we still appear at present to have a natural bias in favor of personal strength and social elitism, and against personal similarity and social equality. But with the light of reason, we can easily and clearly recognize that cultural traditions long predicated upon patriarchy and paternalism are inherently unjust, because they facilitate and perpetuate the natural tendency of the strong to secure, and consequently to be granted, access to most of the social advantages, and of the weak to be denied access to the same. This ancient cultural phenomenon is illusory, however, because those who appear to be strong may actually be weak, or may eventually succumb to weakness, while those who appear to be weak may actually be strong, or may eventually grow in strength. Accordingly, we can only repudiate any interpretation of social justice, no matter how dignified by precedent and tradition, which is so patently unfair.

5. THE PROBLEMS OF CONSERVATISM DURING A PERIOD OF SOCIAL DYSFUNCTION AND OF LIBERALISM DURING A PERIOD OF SOCIAL WELL-BEING

Both conservatism and liberalism are commonly associated with democracy today, as indeed they should be, since they constitute the two predominant political philosophies which provide the bases of, and guidance for, the various active political parties which in turn conceptualize and implement relevant public policy. Conservatives comprise those citizens who are generally satisfied with the present state of society (whenever society is reasonably prosperous and functionally effective) inasmuch as they have attained an adequate and satisfactory measure of personal success, affluence, and happiness throughout the courses of their lives within, and by means of, a social environment that has largely been protective of, and facilitative for, their various personal interests and activities. When the life of the society mirrors the lives of its conservative citizens so that there is, in general, an adequate measure of security, prosperity, and well-being for all or most of the members of society, then it can correctly be said that the conservative weltanschauung is appropriate and that political action should be taken to maintain a stable society so that the various successful personal accomplishments of the recent past can be made to continue without interruption at least into the near future. Alternatively, liberals comprise those citizens who are generally dissatisfied with the present state of society (whenever society is unevenly prosperous and is functionally effective only for citizens who belong to privileged social classes) because the social environment does not protect and assist the weaker members of society as it does those who are able to demonstrate accumulated wealth and past personal success. Such "weaker members of society" include not only those adults who may be disadvantaged or underprivileged but also those who may have succumbed to personal disability (as a consequence of chronic illness or a serious injury) or economic hardship (through no fault of their own), over and above those who are very young and those who are very old. When the actual life of the society mirrors the social critique of its liberal citizens so that there is, in general, an inadequate and undesirable measure of security, prosperity, and well-being for all or most of the members of society (or, stated in another way, for a substantial and progressively increasing portion of society), then it can also be correctly said that the liberal weltanschauung is appropriate and that political action should be taken to change the conditions of society so that its unjust features can be eliminated through corrective legislation and public policy.

Having identified the appropriate phases for either conservative or liberal political leadership and action within the recurring cycles of socioeconomic activity in a democracy, it will not be our purpose at this time to develop a comprehensive discussion of the merits and faults of the two political philosophies. Instead, we simply wish to acknowledge the obvious *absurdities* which arise when a liberal political policy is adopted during a period of social well-being (because the economic costs and disruptions associated with unnecessary sociopolitical change can quickly and easily create an impediment and a detriment to social well-being), and when a conservative political policy is adopted during a period of social dysfunction (because the sociopolitical changes which could have been implemented to eliminate obvious social injustice will have been deliberately and effectively prevented, and the social dysfunction that had already commenced will inevitably become worse).

6. The Problem of Deficit Financing

The correct and appropriate functions of government in a democratic society are to achieve the optimal equilibrium between personal freedom and social justice. These functions can be classified into either of two general categories. The first category comprises the functions which address the essential needs of particular persons who are severely disadvantaged for a portion of their lifetimes (as compared with the average members of society): the need which children and adolescents have for education so that they can become productive and self-sufficient adult members of society; the need which various persons—the disabled, the chronically ill (including the mentally ill), the victims of natural and man-made disasters, the victims of crime—have either for temporary public financial assistance or for lifelong public subsistence income and supportive services; the need which the elderly have for public retirement subsistence income and medical care. The second category comprises the functions which address the needs of all of the citizens for a secure, viable, and healthy natural and social environment: providing personal security (with respect both to one's person and one's property) by means of the police and the military; developing, maintaining, and improving the public infrastructure; protecting the natural environment against natural and man-made abuse by means of the enactment and enforcement of relevant legislation; regulating the economy to achieve the optimal equilibrium between personal freedom and social justice, likewise by means of the enactment and enforcement of relevant legislation.

Now, financing the costs of the functions of government in a democratic society can be accomplished in either of two ways: by taxation or by sovereign debt. Whether accomplished through financial equity (taxation, inasmuch as all of the members of a democratic society are the owners of the government of their society) or through financial obligation (sovereign debt), the financing of the functions which will either provide financial assistance for particular disadvantaged persons or maintain a secure, viable, and healthy natural and social environment for all of the people—without necessarily facilitating future income generation in the private sector of the economy—will correspondingly impoverish most of the members of society: such is the necessary cost of providing these essential benefits to society. It should not be very difficult for everyone to recognize that the values of such benefits greatly exceed their costs: accordingly, the imposition of such costs by the government is just. If the impoverishment occurs through taxation, then the members of society will have less of their own money to spend in their private financial affairs; if through sovereign debt, then they will be paying higher prices in their private financial affairs—since the money which will have been created by the government to finance activities which can never help to generate income in the private sector of the economy will certainly create inflation. If these financial detriments can be contained within the current fiscal period, then all is fair: society will have accepted and paid the costs of providing equitable and necessary social benefits in the same fiscal period during which the benefits were provided. However, this can only happen by means of taxation, as when the government practices balanced budgeting such that the operating costs of government never exceed the revenues of government within a given fiscal period. If the financial detriments of which we have been speaking are *not* contained within the current fiscal period—as when they arise by means of sovereign debt—then all is *not* fair, because society must bear the burden of this debt in subsequent fiscal periods. At such time that the debt *is* paid, the impoverishment that had been created upon its incursion will disappear, since the expenditure for the debt payment will have been offset by a corresponding deflation in prices and the original status quo will have been restored. Until such time, however, the problem of temporal injustice will quickly arise, wherein society will presently confront the same nonproductive social needs as before while simultaneously being obligated to finance the needs of a prior fiscal period.

The proper incursion of sovereign debt is similar to that of debt financing in the private sector, i.e., to finance capital expenditures for public works which will provide benefits to society in future periods and which can be amortized to expense throughout the fiscal periods which will comprise the expected lifetime of the assets which will be so provided; and to facilitate future income generation in the private sector by means of investments in education and public infrastructure. Whenever annual budgetary deficits are entirely or largely cancelled out by occasional budgetary surpluses over the course of a decade or a generation, deficit financing of the costs of providing equitable and necessary (but nonproductive) social benefits will not present a moral problem to society, but whenever budgetary deficits gradually accumulate to a substantial sum after the passage of a decade or a generation, they create an obvious problem of temporal injustice. Furthermore, although they may facilitate the generation of future revenues in the private sector of the economy, the *routine* costs of providing public education or of maintaining the public infrastructure cannot truly be said to comprise the kinds of capital expenditures which justify the incursion of sovereign debt. Consequently, we can only affirm the sound principle and unqualified practice of balanced budgeting in the financing of the costs of operations of the government in a democratic society.

IV.   IN ECONOMICS

We have previously acknowledged the ascendence of reason over the more primitive forces of nature in human affairs, and we have likewise acknowledged (as a necessary corollary of our prime observation) the ascendence of democracy over oligarchy in politics. As we engage in a discussion of illusionary suppositions and false premises which are extant in the realm of economic matters, we feel compelled to begin by acknowledging the ascendence of two dichotomous economic ideologies in modern history which have largely supplanted the earlier primitive economic systems that are generally associated with the oligarchies of the past. We are talking now, of course, about the ascendence of capitalism and socialism over feudalism and mercantilism. Since capitalism essentially represents the private economic interests of the members of society while socialism represents the collective interests, some accommodation and collaboration between the two advanced economic ideologies appears both necessary and inevitable for the eventual emergence of an optimal economic ideology to operate in tandem with democracy, and the evidence of such accomodative and collaborative efforts can already be clearly seen today in either of these two approaches to the laying down of a sound and effective economic system for a modern democratic society. Conversely, it is equally apparent that neither approach in its original, pure, and mutually exclusive form can ever remain viable (let alone optimal) for a modern democratic society.

It is our present purpose, then, to expose the deficiencies of either approach where they fail to admit and to utilize the essential and necessary features of the other and, in keeping with an admitted bias toward the personal, private, and subjective dimension of human experience, to propose as a paradigm of the optimal economic system for a democratic society the model of a modified capitalistic system (specifically, the model of regulated capitalism in a democracy). This model which we are proposing, however, is not in itself entirely free from certain misconceptions and illusions, and we will attempt in due turn to shine some light upon these as well, with the hope of facilitating the recognition and avoidance of the most probable pitfalls which inevitably will straddle the course of its successful implementation and fulfillment. Let us continue now with a brief discussion of the fundamental problem of capitalism when it is *not* regulated by the government on behalf of the common welfare of all of the members of society, which is to say, when a democratic society has adopted and legitimized laissez-faire capitalism as its economic ideology.

1. THE PROBLEMS OF MONOPOLY AND OLIGOPOLY

The fundamental problem of laissez-faire capitalism is its tendency to promote economic imperialism. While it is firmly predicated on the supposition that desirable and necessary economic transactions which take place in free markets can and will determine optimal economic consequences, experience has demonstrated that it has often yielded suboptimal effects. To be specific, there are certain economic sectors and certain industries in which it is possible for a small number of players to subvert this otherwise excellent economic ideological system through the stratagem of securing complete control over the means of production, distribution, and marketing, thereby establishing oligopoly or even monopoly. Let us digress briefly to conceptualize how it is that this economic phenomenon is so detrimental.

Let us hypothesize 10,000 participants in one sector of the economy. The participants are organized into 100 companies of 100 employees. All of the companies manufacture and sell widgets. Some of the companies manufacture high quality widgets and sell them at a relatively high price, some manufacture low quality widgets and sell them at a low price, and some manufacture medium quality widgets which sell at a median price. Various other factors also differentiate the companies, such as a particular choice of raw materials, of product design and production process, of distribution channels, of advertising and promotional techniques. Now, if 10 companies should find a way together to secure complete control of access to all of the raw materials which are necessary to manufacture this product, then they can sell their widgets at a price substantially greater than the price of even the relatively high priced widgets, thereby—to the extent of this price differential—enriching themselves while slightly impoverishing all of the consumers of widgets throughout the general population as well as greatly impoverishing the other 9,000 participants until they find viable alternative products to manufacture and to sell.

If this example of economic imperialism such as we have just described should be extended to many other sectors of the economy so that several oligopolies and monopolies inevitably emerge throughout the general economy, the effect will be to impoverish the majority of consumers in the general population to a substantial extent while at the same time substantially enriching the minority of producers who are engaged in oligopoly and monopoly. Eventually, the middle class will erode and disappear, to be replaced by a small upper class and a large lower class. Of course, this general effect was correctly predicted by Karl

Marx in Europe during the 19th century. However, Marx did *not* foresee that democratic societies might possess the rational capacity to formulate and to implement a critical self-corrective economic policy.

Modern democracies have opposed the detrimental effect of laissez-faire capitalism such as we have been describing by introducing legislation to regulate the economy sufficiently to prevent most monopolies and to place constraints on oligopolies in such industries where the forces of capital investment and the operation of economies of scale favor their presence. The consequential modification of laissez-faire capitalism is commonly known as regulated capitalism, and while considerable debate persists at the present time as to the extent to which government should be involved in regulating the economy of a democratic society, we submit that there is unanimous incontrovertible agreement among most rational citizens that the aforementioned problems of monopoly and oligopoly demand at least that some modest level of governmental regulation is absolutely essential, and furthermore that the periodic calls for a restoration of the conditions of laissez-faire capitalism are totally untenable.

2. THE PROBLEMS OF COMMUNISM AND SOCIALISM

Regulated capitalism, once it has sufficiently modified laissez-faire capitalism so that it cannot be captured and subverted to any substantial extent by a few wealthy and influential economic players, permits the maximum degree of personal freedom for all of the participants in the economy of a democratic society. With the exception of some small degree of governmental regulation of the economy—to the extent that such regulation must be continuously maintained in order to prevent the problems of monopoly and oligopoly such as we have previously discussed—regulated capitalism permits each economic player to choose the particular kind of work which one can best perform in order to contribute to the general economic production, as well as to choose the particular goods and services which one must obtain for the optimal satisfaction of one's specific personal needs and desires. In the sphere of economic justice (in contradistinction to that of economic freedom), we would further argue that regulated capitalism, which has long been and still remains in direct competition with the economic ideologies of communism and socialism, permits the maximum degree of social justice for all of the participants in the economy of a democratic society. This is so because of the inherent contradictions within these two ideologies which espouse the supremacy of justice in economic affairs. These contradictions deny the permanent effectiveness and practicability of communism and socialism (unless the latter has been substantially modified so as to be compatible with the requirements of democracy). Let us now attempt to indicate the contradictions within these ideologies in turn.

Communism is the fusion of socialism and totalitarianism. Therein, of course, resides its essential contradiction—because while the *economic* ideology, socialism, provides optimal social justice, the *political* ideology, totalitarianism, to which socialism is fused and through which socialism is totally controlled, produces social injustice. Let us state this paradox in slightly different words. A totalitarian state is essentially an oligarchy, and an oligarchy inevitably produces oligopoly or monopoly.

When socialism operates in a democracy, it is generally promoted by social-democratic political parties which must compete with various nonsocialist political parties in an attempt to attain political dominance. Whenever social-democratic political parties *do* succeed in attaining political dominance, their tenures will generally only be temporary whenever their administrations should encounter economic difficulties, because the nonsocialist political parties will then be reinstated. Under socialism, the means of economic production and distribution are controlled by the government for the common benefit of all of the members of society—either through public ownership and public enterprise or through extensive public regulation of private ownership and private enterprise. If socialism involves public ownership, such ownership may be maximal, medial, or minimal. To the extent that such public ownership may be maximal or even medial, the inevitable reversions of public ownership which continually arise as a consequence of periodic alternations of political dominance between social-democratic political parties and nonsocialist political parties create enormous economic instability and dysfunction. Accordingly, anything greater than minimal public ownership will ultimately be ineffective and impracticable in the economy of a democratic society.

On the other hand, if socialism involves minimal or no public ownership, and alternatively relies upon extensive public regulation of private ownership and private enterprise, then economic disruptions occasioned by reversions when opposition parties return to power will neither be intolerable nor insurmountable. We submit that continuous debate (with respect to an optimal social vision and an optimal public policy) between the social-democratic political parties on the one side and the nonsocialist political parties on the other side in any democracy are both healthy and necessary for the development and fulfillment of an optimal economy for the society. We also acknowledge that socialism which operates in a democracy still requires and involves *some* degree of public economic planning and public social engineering. These activities can only be effectively carried out by an elite group of experienced professionals who possess extensive theoretical and practical expertise in economics, political science, and sociology, serving as elected or appointed representatives of all of the people on behalf of the common well-being of all of the members of society. It is both appropriate and desirable that the theoretical objectives and policy initiatives of such an elite group be continually reviewed, evaluated, and then either accepted or rejected by opposition political parties so that the will of the majority of the members of society can be continuously reflected in the shaping and realizing of a viable and optimal economy. To attain the equilibrium between freedom and justice in the economic affairs of a democracy, we have identified and affirmed the services of the economic ideology of regulated capitalism for providing an optimal mixed-market economy, and we have further

intimated that regulated capitalism is at once the logical and practical consequence of the accumulated and channeled interests and efforts of the social-
democratic political parties which have been operating to advance socialist ideas, priorities, and objectives in democratic societies. The present discussion requires some further elucidation, which now follows.

3. THE PROBLEMS STILL PERSISTING UNDER REGULATED CAPITALISM IN A DEMOCRACY

If we can agree that the optimal economy for a democratic society must permit
and provide an equilibrium between freedom and justice in the economic affairs
of the society, and if we can also agree that regulated capitalism is the only economic ideology which can provide such an equilibrium, then we should be able
to conclude without too much difficulty that regulated capitalism is the optimal
economic ideology for a democratic society. The only great difficulty which
remains, of course, is the problem of locating and arriving at such an equilibrium, since those who favor freedom in economic matters will not be willing to
accept as great a loss of economic freedom in the course of attaining economic
justice as those who favor justice. Furthermore, if those who favor freedom in
economic matters begin to feel in any respect that the attempt to attain economic
justice is *itself* unjust, then they will refuse to participate in the effort and they
may also do all that they can do to frustrate and to defeat it. This eventuality
leads us directly to the first of the problems which still persist under regulated
capitalism in a democracy.

(a) The Problem of Reversion

Reversion is an act or a process of returning to a former condition such
as may have been in place before a recent change was enacted. We have previously noted the problem of reversion which often arises when the pendulum of
political power swings between the social-democratic political parties and the
nonsocialist political parties, because the conservatives commonly desire (espe-
cially during times of adversity) to weaken or to nullify many of the advances in
social and economic justice which have been slowly and steadily achieved by
the liberals on behalf of the general well-being of the society. Let us not fail to
remember that, in essence, the conservatives believe that social well-being and
economic prosperity can best be achieved through personal initiative and private
enterprise, while the liberals believe that some level of public initiative and collective effort must be undertaken to provide social and economic justice, not
only for disadvantaged and underprivileged individuals and minorities but for *all*
individuals at such times when they may be physically or mentally disabled, or
otherwise they may be furthest from the time of the prime of life within their
own lifespans (as when they are very young or very old). Consequently, the conservatives believe that the functions of government should be limited to one or

two, such as to provide security for individuals in their social affairs and perhaps also to construct and to maintain a common infrastructure of communication, transportation, sanitation, water supply, energy utilities, and related public works within society. Alternatively, the liberals believe in several other functions of government beyond those approved by the conservatives, such as universal public education for the young; universal public financial assistance for the elderly; universal insurance to indemnify individuals who might suffer personal injury as a consequence of natural disasters or of hazardous occupations; environmental protection; and economic regulation. The dialectics of democracy suggest that the course of future progress may be fractious and lengthy and that it may inevitably involve a substantial degree of vacillation and experimentation. It appears more probable (and somewhat more hopeful simply because it is obviously so necessary) that a reasonably steady course of compromise and reciprocal influence will ultimately provide a coherent common vision of how best to conserve, to protect, and to improve the natural environment and also of how best to build and to sustain an excellent social environment, so that, as a consequence, the social dysfunction and instability which is continually occasioned by the recurring problem of reversion will disappear altogether as democratic societies achieve permanent social well-being and economic prosperity.

With respect to economic matters, the great obstacle in the course of progress toward the objective of attaining permanent economic justice is the reluctance of the conservatives to accept the necessity of public economic regulation. The immediate critical task of the liberals must be to convince the conservatives of this necessity. Once this task has been successfully completed, the dynamic interaction between the elected and appointed representatives of the two competitive politico-economic weltanschauungen can determine the location of the equilibrium between freedom and justice. At this point, the remaining problems which still persist under regulated capitalism in a democracy will come into sharp focus. Let us now consider them in turn.

(b) The Problem of Official Corruption

As we have observed, the conservatives believe that social problems are best solved through the cumulative private initiatives of the most determined, energetic, and capable members of society (who act primarily in their individual self-interest and only secondarily in the greater interest of the whole society) and they further believe that if this point of view cannot succeed, that no alternative one can ever be possible. This is so because they believe that human accomplishment essentially comes about through the qualities, interests, plans, and activities of superior individuals and not as the product of common effort in realizing common interests; they further believe that the latter point of view will always be impossible because the best people will refuse to subvert their own interests and objectives to those of the common welfare, and few among the mediocre masses will ever rise to provide effective leadership for the task. The conservatives essentially are elitists and they all hold in common an unfavorable and highly pessimistic opinion of human nature, of human potential, of the possibility of universal human individual and collective self-actualization. As a consequence, the conservatives do not believe that governmental activity can provide social justice because the officials who might be entrusted to regulate economic affairs for the common welfare would generally find a way to abuse their power for their personal advantage, and even if this objection could occasionally be overcome, the majority of people will always remain too base, too pernicious, and too dishonest even to deserve social justice.

Accordingly, the task at hand of the liberals must be to demonstrate effectively the enormous error of the conservative political weltanschauung. First, let us engage the problem of official corruption. We should be able to recognize that this problem is simply a function of the problem of personal dishonesty, because if most people are essentially dishonest, then public officials who are elected or appointed from their number will inevitably become corrupt. On the other hand, if we can successfully argue that most people are *not* essentially dishonest, then public officials who are elected or appointed from their number can only become corrupt if they are provided access to power which they would otherwise never attain, despite which the objectivity and transparency of public service generally provides adequate safeguards either to prevent or to expose and then to eliminate official corruption. We cannot satisfactorily dismiss our discussion of the problem of official corruption, then, until we consider the problem of personal dishonesty.

(c) The Problem of Personal Dishonesty

Truth is the foundation of wisdom. Truth has two dimensions: objective and subjective. Empiricism is solely concerned with objective truth: it provides all of the knowledge contained in the various sciences. Ethics is concerned both with objective truth—as it specifically concerns optimal human cooperation—and subjective truth: it provides the knowledge that enables personal integrity and social harmony.

Personal integrity is neither all that easy to attain nor to maintain. It requires not only knowledge but a steadfast commitment to practice that which has been learned. Since the attainment of personal integrity comprises an internalization of truth—comprising, as it were, a marriage between person and truth—it has, like truth itself, two dimensions: objective and subjective. The objective dimension involves a personal attitude of care for *others,* including benevolence, courtesy, good faith, fair play, support for justice, and an absence of personal dishonesty. The subjective dimension involves a personal attitude of care for *oneself,* including self-examination, self-interest, self-respect, a motivation toward self-sufficiency, a further motivation toward self-fulfillment, and an absence of self-deception.

The present time approaches the high noon of the day of the species. The conservatives—who look backwards in time and who worship the past— readily recognize all that is primitive and bestial in the species and so they honor only the great heroes who throughout history have done the most to discipline themselves and to advance the species. The liberals—who look forward in time and who place their hope in the future—readily recognize all that is potential and noble in the species and so they honor all that is good in the species, whenever and wherever they can find it. Unlike the conservatives, who see only the dark underside of the human coin, the liberals understand that the morning of the particular will quickly give way to the afternoon of the universal, the morning of specific heterogeneity to the afternoon of specific homogeneity, the morning of nature to the afternoon of reason. With respect to the public regulation of capitalism in a democracy, the problem of personal dishonesty—because of which sufficient public revenues from taxation can never be collected, adequate barriers against unjust personal financial aggrandizement can never be erected, and subsistent financial assistance for disadvantaged and underprivileged members of society can never be constantly sustained until such time that an incontrovertibly just society can be permanently established—will then no longer present the insurmountable obstacle which it had almost always previously imposed throughout the late morning of the species. A crucial modification of human nature can occur within the near future by means of a new, deliberate, and comprehensive program of universal acculturation providing a transmutation of the biological urge toward self-preservation to an emerging self-awareness of personal obligation (and, as an essential and unavoidable corollary, of personal dishonor—which will thenceforth always be associated with unethical and immoral personal behavior). The central components of this new social policy must include the adoption of a universal standard of morality, the enactment and enforcement of a universal body of law, and the introduction of, and continuous provision for, universal moral education, once the disparate democracies of earth join together to form one common world democratic community. With an effective, yet not unfriendly, resistance to the skepticism and opposition of the conservatives, the courageous present task of the liberals must be to lead the species into a better, happier, and more enlightened future.

V.   IN PERSONAL AFFAIRS

Thus far, we have considered the effects of faulty beliefs in the realm of social affairs: in religion, in politics, and in economics. On the whole, with respect to religion, we have observed: (1), that it is obsolete; (2), that its continuing presence and influence in human affairs generally creates more difficulty for human beings than any particular assistance in life which it may be seen to provide; and (3), that the entire realm of ethics should henceforth be set apart from religion so that it can better be utilized and advanced in a wholly rational manner for universal human well-being. With respect to politics and economics, where a nexus with human reality is much more obvious, we have carefully differentiated between ideologies which conform closely with truth (which is to say, those which appear clearly to promote optimal human interpersonal and social well-being) and those which do not.

At this juncture, we will turn to examine the effects of faulty or illusory thinking in the realm of personal affairs, admittedly a more difficult exercise since we will soon be departing from the world of objectivity in an earnest attempt to penetrate and to explore the world of subjectivity. The initial stage of our journey will consider various beliefs and values which have little connection with the ideologies that are prominent in the realm of social affairs but which are commonly held to be necessary for personal success and happiness. Since they have arisen as a consequence of common observations, we may say that they are objective. Subsequently, however, we must enter a world that will be difficult enough for any of us to navigate at any given time with any feeling of sustainable satisfaction, the world of subjectivity, a world of uncertainty that is ever fraught with a succession of disappointing illusions and perplexing ambiguities. To the extent that any of us can successfully navigate this world, the singular world of our inner self, we will learn at once how best to be free and how best to be happy.

1. INVOLVING QUESTIONABLE BELIEFS AND VALUES

To begin our discussion of the effects of illusions in the conduct of our personal affairs, we must digress momentarily to distinguish between an illusion held by an entire population and an illusion held only by particular individuals or sub-populations within that population. For example, Europeans believed in the Ptolemaic geocentric theory of the universe until the ascendence of the Copernican heliocentric theory in modern history. We can say *now*, then, that the theory of Ptolemy is false and that the theory of Copernicus is true. Consequently, we can also say now that—with respect to an understanding of the universe and until the time of Copernicus—Europeans were ignorant and that their belief in a geocentric universe was an illusion. Consequently again, we can acknowledge that—with respect to the natural world which we encounter and interpret through our common experience and objectivity—ignorance is one's thinking under an illusion while knowledge is one's acceptance of the incontrovertible conclusions of science. Universal knowledge, then, never becomes universal ignorance and illusion unless at some time in the future it is superseded by new and contradictory knowledge. Knowledge, then, may either be absolute because we have already obtained the truth and the truth will never change, or it may be relative because at the present we lack sufficient tools to obtain the truth. In the latter case, we may all be presently thinking under an illusion without our knowing that we may be doing so. In the former case, on the other hand, some persons will not be in possession of absolute knowledge because those persons—through lack of sufficient soundness of mind, intelligence, education, or experience—will fail to grasp it. Such persons also, then, may presently and alternatively be thinking under an illusion without their fully understanding that they may be doing so.

To return to the object of our present consideration, that is, to consider illusions involving our personal affairs, let us now attempt to identify and to evaluate the various beliefs and values which are commonly held to be necessary for personal success and happiness. If we should be successful, then we should be able to distinguish between those which are true and those which are false. Some of the beliefs and values will generally fall into either of two categories: those which are egocentric and one in particular which is altruistic. Those which are egocentric are anticipated primarily to provide benefits for the value holder and only secondarily, indirectly, or unintentionally to provide benefits for others. The converse is true for the belief and value which is altruistic. As with our previous discussion of the dichotomy between freedom and justice in political and economic affairs, and the optimality of achieving an equilibrium between the two extremes, we will find that those personal beliefs and values are optimal which tend to promote a balance of benefits between each person and the aggregate of all of the other members of the society to which each person belongs.

We admit that our list of common beliefs and values, relevant as it may be in any democratic society today even remotely resembling the United States of

America, may not be fully comprehensive or all-inclusive but it is hoped that any beliefs and values which may come to mind that are not included in the list will at once be found to be subcultural, countercultural, or foreign vis-à-vis those which can be found to be commonly held throughout the general population. Our list must certainly include the following: pleasure, fame, wealth, power, freedom, justice, love, knowledge, stability, moderation, rebellion, humor, and beauty. Some of these beliefs and values are held by persons within such a large and broad division of society that their proper designation and classification cannot truly be considered to be subcultural. For example, the value of stability is commonly esteemed by persons who are politically conservative and it is likewise commonly esteemed by elderly persons who have retired and are living on fixed incomes. The value of rebellion is commonly esteemed in varying degrees of intensity by adolescents and young adults until they have individually formulated clear concepts of selfhood, of society, and of an integration of selfhood and society.

Freedom and justice are closely related concepts although they appear to be diametrically opposed to each other. Free people living in a just social environment will scarcely be aware of either of these values; people without freedom living in an unjust social environment will come to understand and consequently to adhere to both of them. Apart from this general observation, of course, specific instances may be particularly complicated. A person without freedom may live in an unjust family that is itself present within an otherwise just society: such a person, then, will come to esteem freedom. Another person without freedom may live as a member of a happy family but also as a member of an oppressed minority within an unjust society: such a person, then, will come to esteem both freedom and justice, and if that person should ever attain a sufficient measure of personal freedom, nonetheless he or she will continue to esteem and to seek justice.

In varying degrees, all of the beliefs and values which we are considering are universal because they involve both the development of personhood and the development of society. The ones which we have already discussed are the most fundamental: without an optimal equilibrium between personal freedom and social justice, no *democratic* society can be strong or its citizens happy. From a social perspective, the value of rebellion is closely associated with that of justice, and the value of stability is identified with the preservation of the society which has once attained an optimal equilibrium between freedom and justice. From a personal perspective, the value of rebellion appears to be quite necessary during the earlier stages of a person's lifespan, when the person is finding and establishing his or her unique identity and individuality, during the process of which the person often feels compelled to question (and sometimes even to forsake for an indeterminate period) all that which has been taught to him or to her by others that has been deemed necessary for the person to live a satisfactory, full, and worthy life, and during the course of which the person actually does rebel to a greater or lesser extent so that he or she can gradually internalize and eventually come to terms with such knowledge, primarily by means of the immediate and unexpected difficulties, trials, and crises of personal experience. From a personal perspective, the value of stability appears to be equally necessary during the later stages of a person's lifespan, when the person has at last firmly established his or her unique identity, when the rate of personal growth has decreased considerably because the person has already attained all or most of his or her personal goals, and when the person in consequence desires to sustain for as long as possible the kind of life which he or she has carefully created for himself or herself.

We will find that certain others among the beliefs and values which are relevant in the pursuit of our personal affairs and which remain for our consideration are equally valid as the ones which we have already discussed. These will include the following: knowledge, moderation, humor, beauty, and love.

It is neither necessary for our present object now to engage in an epistemological discussion nor to recount the major events denoting the ascendance of empiricism in modern history. We will assume that no one will deny the supremacy of truth over falsehood or of knowledge over ignorance, and that everyone will acknowledge at once the ultimate triumph of empiricism in human thought and the supreme value of truth and knowledge in the satisfactory conduct of human affairs. Inasmuch as truth is a specific *quality* or *criterion* of knowledge, we are considering truth and knowledge together as an undivided human value. Knowledge is also very closely associated with judgment (which we will presently discuss in greater detail) inasmuch as a person must possess a sufficiency of knowledge in order to evaluate various concepts, processes, and behaviors, or to determine the better and the best of various competitive alternatives of merit.

"Meden agan" ("nothing in excess") is one of the great universal moral aphorisms which have flourished in human history and this time-honored precept has been passed down to us from the ancient Greeks. Our exercise of sound judgment requires us to avoid extremes of moral behavior. With respect to the intentionality of moral conduct, we are quite simply talking about our discovery and adoption of the medial position between two opposing concepts, principles, or conditions, either of which possess obvious intrinsic merit, as between individualism and collectivism, between self-realization and social cohesion, between egoism and altruism, between freedom and justice, or between candor and tact. We are *not* talking about any decision toward *mediocrity*, which may occur when we choose the medial position between two opposing concepts, principles, or conditions of which only *one* possesses obvious intrinsic merit, as between good and evil or between excellence and unworthiness. In the early days of recorded human thought, Plato determined that it should be necessary for human beings to possess four virtues in order to enjoy a good life: wisdom (which is to say, prudence, discernment, or judgment), temperance, courage, and justice. Aristotle agreed with Plato as to the necessity of the four virtues but in addition he advocated a choice of the mean between extremes within each of these virtues: such mean is most obvious in justice (where one must choose an outcome for a contested issue or transaction which will benefit and satisfy both of the

antagonists) and in wisdom (where one must attempt to avoid uncertainties and dilemmas when making personal decisions); in courage, the mean is situated between cowardice and rashness in one's reaction to hardship or danger; in temperance, between self-indulgence and abstinence in one's experience of the pleasures of the senses. Throughout all of the preceding comments, we can see that the concept of moderation is primarily employed in connection with sound thinking and balanced judgment. In this sense, it is a quality or criterion of truth and as such it is simply an appropriate component of the value of knowledge which we have previously discussed. Consequently, it is only when the concept of moderation is employed in connection with one's experience and enjoyment of the pleasures of the senses—whether those of nourishment, of intoxication, or of sexual gratification—that we can consider it as a value in its own right, and it is in this sense that we so do at this time. Our concluding comment with respect to the value of moderation concurs with traditional opinion: that some enjoyment of the pleasures of the senses is natural, desirable, and good—providing that the same is not carried out to an extent that causes harm to others or permanent and irreparable harm to oneself.

In the constant effort which each person exerts to maximize the pleasures of life and to minimize the pains, a wide variety of strategies are employed. As mammals, and more specifically as primates, human beings have evolved with certain powerful biological predispositions, salient among which is an inclination to be sociable; to maintain close and enduring relationships with members of one's family: both of the family into which one has been born and the family which one may have established with some other person (usually some person *outside* of the family into which one has been born, whom one has chosen as a mate); and to cooperate with other people in productive endeavors of various kinds which provide benefits for all of the participants. The emotion most commonly associated with this natural affinity between the members of a human family is *love* and the consequent conceptualization of this emotion gives rise to the value of love. The value of love holds that that behavior is right that helps other persons to satisfy their needs and to avert or to alleviate their hurts. This value is rooted in the moral principle of beneficial reciprocity. To the extent at least that it involves the condition and quality of interpersonal relationships primarily within the social unit most closely associated with the reproductive function, love, both as an emotion and as a value, is common among most of the members of the species. Love is somewhat less common when it is extended to include all of the members of the species, where it is known as *altruism* and where it must become an ideology as well as a value and an emotion, such as we find in certain religions like Buddhism and Christianity or in certain ancient Chinese philosophies like Confucianism and Moism. We can only acknowledge, affirm, and sanction the obvious happiness which arises from human love; consequently, we can find no fault with love, neither as a personal value nor as a social ideology.

The value of humor normally emerges from, and is dependent upon, the value of love. Let us now attempt to explain this statement. Because we are able to love others, we are also able to have sympathy for others, and when we learn of the misfortune of others but at the same time we are unable to help them, we experience considerable anxiety and unhappiness. If our anticipation of pain during the course of our apprehension of some narration concerning the misfortune of others should abruptly terminate as the narration suddenly turns to absurdity, we experience an abrupt release of psychic tension resulting in laughter and relief. We then immediately realize that the narration was about a fictitious event concerning fictitious people and that the narrator has deliberately created a well-intentioned deception for us in order to allow us to enjoy the enormous relief and pleasure which always arises whenever anticipated trouble disappears. To be a little more specific, let us say that humor relieves us of the obligation which we feel toward others (because of the emotion of love) by engaging our rapt attention and then dissolving it in absurdity. Humor arouses a sense of personal obligation to someone and then abruptly relieves the stress and discomfort which proceed from our anxiety to fulfill the obligation. The resulting cessation of painful sensation and concurrent explosion of pleasure provokes laughter and delight. Since, in the end, human existence can never be perfect but only optimal, the value of humor will always be useful, desirable, and beneficial for human beings as a supplementary, albeit artificial, source of happiness.

Beauty is a conceptualization of a perception which serves as a symbol of either a satisfaction of need or a security from hurt and which simulates a sensation of pleasure and a feeling of happiness. The value of beauty, then, involves a deliberate attempt to seek and to enjoy beauty. Such beauty may be either natural or artistic. In the case of natural beauty, a person may appreciate beauty in human beings as well as in other natural phenomena. We have powerful biological predispositions to seek and to enjoy beauty in other human beings, particularly among those from which we might select a mate, since human beauty generally indicates good health and biological fitness for procreation. Likewise, an appreciation of the beauty of a natural setting may suggest a parcel of land which is desirable to possess because it is fertile and consequently valuable for producing food and for sustaining human habitation. In other instances of natural beauty, as well as in all instances in the case of artistic beauty, an appreciation of beauty serves in a less direct manner as a *symbol* of satisfaction of need or of security from hurt. Obviously, an appreciation of beauty will be of little value wherever human beings are reduced to a daily struggle for survival and subsistence, but once human beings have satisfied their most critical immediate needs, the value of beauty, like the value of humor, will always be useful, desirable, and beneficial as a supplementary source of happiness. Moderation in the enjoyment of either cognitive function is the optimal course of conduct: if a person enjoys humor to excess, that person will often become frivolous and will not likely remain sufficiently serious to satisfy the requirements of life; if a person enjoys beauty to excess, that person will often become insatiable and will likely be neglectful of ethics to a considerable extent, having little regard, and creating much trouble, for oneself as well as for others, like the Seducer in Kierkegaard's *Either/Or*.

We have affirmed—whether in general but with certain qualifications, in specific situations, or in particular stages of the human life span—the various personal values which we have previously discussed. We will presently find more to object to, and in consequence more to qualify, when we consider the four remaining personal values, which we may correctly and appropriately classify as the egoistical personal values inasmuch as they exclusively promote self-serving personal objectives. These include pleasure, fame, wealth, and power.

The value of pleasure holds that that behavior is right which induces, prolongs, and intensifies the sensation of pleasure and which avoids, terminates, or relieves the sensation of pain. No other personal value is so primitive or as fundamental as pleasure; no other personal value is so predicated in proximity and immediacy; no other personal value is so dangerous and detrimental in the absence of reason. This is so because pleasure is a function of need. In a purely biological sense, existence requires hydration, nourishment, the elimination of toxic waste, and a freedom from fatal injury or disease; in addition, human reproduction requires heterosexual copulation. The sensations of discomfort and pain indicate to sentient beings the presence of various existential needs and hurts as they initially occur or subsequently recur in time; the satisfaction of existential needs and the elimination of existential threats give rise to comfort and pleasure.

Two problems become apparent when a person makes a *value* of pleasure (which is to say, when a person pursues a hedonistic life-style). One arises when the person lacks prudence or is otherwise unable and unwilling to take adequate care of oneself. Then surfeit quickly leads to depletion of energy, apathy, and lethargy; in instances of analgesia, to toxicity, sickness, and sometimes even death. The other problem arises when the person holds no other values. Then the person becomes unable to form or to sustain close relationships with other persons or to contribute very much of value to society in general. Accordingly, the value of pleasure must only be viewed as deceptive, detrimental, and morally unacceptable whenever it is not held by a prudent person in combination and connection with the value of moderation.

A small digression at this juncture may serve to provide a fruitful opportunity to offer some general observations on human nature. As members of a typical (as well as the most recent) family within the order of primates, man is quite able to function with equal facility as a solitary individual or as a social animal. Whether the one or the other existential modality should predominate in any given situation which may be considered appears to be primarily dependent upon the influences and effects of acculturation. Generally speaking, man can suppress his individuality to function effectively as a disciplined member of society whenever his particular society has asserted itself against the other societies with which it relates to such an extent that it has either gained sole supremacy over them or at least has acquired some measure of prestige and preeminence among them. Wherever he is not a member of such an aggressive society, he may have more freedom to function as a solitary individual, searching for the means to assert himself against his fellows (within the parameters of the mores of his society) to gain personal benefits and advantages. Using an analogy from the family of cats, in the former instance man is like the social lions; in the latter, like the solitary tigers. Unlike the cats, however, man can easily adapt to whichever existential modality demonstrates the greatest promise for existential success. Whenever a given society is not aggressive toward its neighbors, and whenever the mores of a given society fail to promote a rational balance between personal and collective interests and activities, man is more likely to think and to act as a solitary individual, and as a consequence he is more likely to adopt and to pursue one or another of the egoistical personal values. Whether or not he takes an interest in the hedonistic life-style, he is quite likely to be attracted to fame, wealth, and power. Whether they are adopted and pursued separately or in combination, these three values appear to provide personal benefits and advantages that are generally unavailable to the majority of the members of society.

With fame, an individual attempts to gain the goodwill of other people so that he may become secure from harm or want of any source. To gain fame, the individual must become known to most others within his society, and he must be judged peerless in that for which he is known. Accordingly, he must provide superior performance in a field of endeavor that is very highly esteemed.

Certain difficulties arise when a person chooses to pursue fame. Firstly, he must be truly proficient to the point of superiority over his rivals within his field. If he merely imitates others without offering an adequate measure of originality, of personal creativity, of unique and unprecedented contribution, he will quickly be found out and his initial sensational successes will not continue. Secondly, he must attain fame in a field that provides an essential benefit for other people; if his fame results from activities that merely provide for others an amusement or a diversion, the value of his fame will be vastly inferior and fleeting vis-à-vis that of one who *does* provide an essential benefit. Thirdly, a person who provides an essential benefit for other people is primarily interested in maximizing the full value of his contribution—which only *he* can do through his *own* effort—so that it can become as perfect as it can be, and consequently he is *not* primarily interested in any recognition which he may obtain as a result of his accomplishments. For these three reasons, we may conclude that fame is a false value whenever it is adopted and pursued for its own sake.

Now let us consider the value of wealth. This value opines the personal acquisition of a large quantity of material goods or their equivalent in money. The rudimentary purpose of wealth is to provide the wherewithal for the satisfaction of a person's basic needs or the prevention of his hurts in quantity sufficient to secure him against unemployment or incapacitation. Beyond its rudimentary purpose, wealth generally provides a measure of personal freedom and comfort that is commensurate with its magnitude.

The fundamental problem with wealth resides in its historic opposition to justice. The problem would not arise if all people in the world were wealthy, but neither this phenomenon nor even an illusion of it have ever occurred in human history. Therefore, those who *are* wealthy must constantly protect their wealth from theft by those who are *not* wealthy, by relying upon the laws of the society of which they are members, by acquiring personal power, or through some combination of these two alternatives. Unless wealthy persons can justify their wealth to the remaining members of society, their wealth will be universally viewed as an unfair personal enrichment at the expense of the other members of society: resentment will build, and wealth will be returned to society at large, either through legislation and taxation, or through social pressures for personal charitable contributions to various social institutions and public services. In the oligarchies of the past, it was impossible for persons of wealth not to be persons of power or not to be persons closely allied with persons of power, but in the aftermath of the democratic revolutions which have eliminated these kinds of social arrangements, persons of wealth have been careful to secure some measure of control over the governments of the democratic societies of which they are members to an extent that is adequate to protect their wealth. In short, if a person of wealth in a democratic society today is not also a person of considerable personal power, then such a person must secure sufficient control over the government of the society of which he is a member, either directly or indirectly, through alliances with other wealthy people, to receive assurance that the laws of the society will remain adequate to protect his wealth. Consequently, the value of wealth cannot be considered independently of the value of power. Before we move on to a discussion of the value of power, however, we must mention one other problem concerning wealth, and particularly concerning those who choose to adopt it as a personal value.

The other problem with wealth only arises to the extent that the means for the satisfaction of a person's needs or the prevention of his hurts is essentially dependent not upon the strength of his own efforts but upon the strength of his close relationships with other people. In this case, the person of wealth—understanding that the magnitude of his wealth is already sufficient to support his subsistence and personal development under all contingencies—mistakenly believes that it is also fully sufficient to provide the wherewithal for the satisfaction of all of his needs which are interpersonal in nature, such as his needs for love, acceptance, recognition, friendship, and affiliation. These needs, however, cannot always be fully satisfied by wealth, and in some instances they cannot be satisfied by wealth at all. One person's devotion to another is not contingent upon a purchase. Neither can those persons who hurt us always be appeased by a tribute. Nonetheless, the person of wealth often attempts to deal with others by *making a deal* with others. Sometimes he is successful and sometimes he is not: the positive outcome is largely dependent upon the event that he has been acting in good faith, and that those with whom he has been in such close relationship have likewise been acting in good faith. In summary, then, we can see that wealth is problematic and that the value of wealth is illusory.

Power, with which wealth is often associated, is likewise problematic and the value of power, with which the value of wealth is also often associated, is likewise illusory. Since the value of power is even more dangerous than the value of wealth, our discussion of it must necessarily be more comprehensive and our disapprobation more definitive.

The value of power is a lifelong personal goal which attempts to gain control over other people. Consequently, it is, like fame, a personal value which always has a social context. It is deeply and seemingly almost inextricably rooted in our long-standing human biological heritage. The primitive family structure of our primatial ancestors generally comprised an alpha male who organized the interests and activities of the other family members in such a manner as to bring optimal advantages and benefits to himself, with any spillover benefits accreting to the others, whether individually or collectively, as tolerated members of the social unit. The human biological predilection for power is also apparent as an instinctive predisposition in several other species, most notably among certain mammalian carnivores such as lions and wolves, but two significant differences between humans and lions or between humans and wolves provide hope that we, as a species, are not inevitably predestined by our biological heritage always either to seek power or otherwise to adapt ourselves as best as we can to the pervasive presence, influence, and domination of the powerful persons who live among us. The first difference: we, as a species, are not exclusively carnivores, but omnivores, like many of the other species within the superfamily Hominoidea; the second: we have the capacity of reason, and if we constantly choose to exercise and to cultivate this capacity, it will allow us to attain the optimality of human existence such as will be totally unlike anything ever before experienced or witnessed during the long primordial morning of the species. Consequently, the characteristic social structures of our past—namely, the patriarchical families centered about the vestiges of the primatial alpha males, and the tribal, national, and imperial oligarchies centered about the interests of minority classes of powerful people—may be totally rejected and discarded if we determine that they may not necessarily be the best social structures for our future.

If we resolve at this juncture to engage in a modest measure of collective introspection, we should have little difficulty in arriving at such a conclusion. To begin, let us suggest that the value of power is chosen by those persons who recognize, whether by inference or intuition, *two* facts: one, that they perceive a personal need to control the other persons around themselves—either to fulfill, or to assist in the fulfillment of, their personal needs, or to prevent, or to assist in the prevention of, their personal hurts—and two, that they are confident in their ability, or their probable success in acquiring an ability, to control other people. Everyone, or almost everyone, can recognize the first fact but few the second, inasmuch as most people are not self-conscious that they do indeed possess a sufficient measure of personal superiority over the abilities and merits of other people; consequently, only a few persons choose to adopt for themselves the value of power. For those few who do, wherever the value of power is only a personal value but not a social value, their lives will ultimately be neither successful nor happy, because the fundamental problem with power, like that with wealth, resides in its stark opposition to justice. In a rational world, where those who are naturally weak can learn to improve themselves, to overcome or to compensate for their natural deficiencies, and to develop their latent talents, the injustices perpetrated by those who are naturally strong upon those who are naturally weak come into sharp focus, resentments simmer and rebellions erupt, and conflict is inevitable. On the other hand, if the value of power is a *social* value as well as a personal value (by which we mean, in order to clarify any misunderstanding, that the *personal* value is widely recognized to engender results which will provide substantial benefits for the common well-being of society)—as it has always been throughout the long evolution of Homo sapiens—then those who choose to adopt it as a personal value *will* be happy and successful since others within their social group who lack sufficient personal strength will quickly accept them as leaders to enable the group to prevail against other groups which may be opposing it or competing against it. This historical social phenomenon occurs all the time today, when the traditional social practices of the past in combination with evolved personal predispositions come into direct conflict with the rationally engendered principles, programs, and enterprises of the present. The consequences for humanity have been tragic inasmuch as the fundamental political process in modern history has involved the introduction and development of democracy in the various states and societies of the world. The phenomenology of power was not widely understood and the collision between the past and the present, and between nature and reason, was largely unnoticed. This is why the emergence of democracy in France during the 19th century was so abruptly subverted under Napoleon; it is also why the all-too-brief appearance of democracy in Germany during the time of the Weimar Republic in the early 20th century was likewise abruptly subverted under Hitler. The common memory of the grandeur of ancient imperial Rome vastly overshadowed that of the brief brilliance of ancient democratic Athens, and all hopes for the modern rise of democracy among the great nations of the European continent were doomed from the outset. The world is in constant flux and much has been learned with respect to the benefits of the ideology of democracy and the detriments of the value of power. In a rational world, where collective self-consciousness of the human universal quickly begins to transcend the human particular, the recurrence of such absurdities as the First Empire of France and the Third Reich of Germany will gradually diminish until they finally disappear altogether.

To conclude our discussion of the value of power, we must affirm that we have found it wanting, like the values of pleasure, fame, and wealth, because, in the end, it is self-defeating, having caused so much injustice, so much grave injury to other people, so much chaos in the human community, that the sweepy aftermath of relentless outcries for justice ultimately crescendos to overpower power itself. In a world that is rational, in a world in which the universal transcends the particular, in a world of equals, in a world in which it is commonly recognized that the best discipline is self-discipline, in a world where democratic government employs a system of checks and balances so that no tier, branch, or agency of government secures excessive or disproportionate power over the others, in a world in which the concept of the value of power is supplanted by the concept of the value of *a balance of power*, the exercise of power will be harmless, minimal, and invisible, and a common consciousness of it virtually absent. In such a world, the unconstrained potentiality for universal peace, social well-being, and personal self-realization shall have finally attained actuality.

Our examination of the effects of faulty thinking in connection with the more common beliefs and values which influence the conduct of our personal affairs now coming to a close, let us directly proceed to discussions by turns of the effects of faulty thinking as it may concern our choices and conduct of our personal occupations and relationships. We believe that illusory introspection with respect to our affiliations and pursuits in these areas creates even greater difficulties for human beings than all of that which we have previously considered.

2. INVOLVING WORK

As we engage in our present discussion, the most important factor to keep always in mind is the concept of *change*. We see change and its effects throughout the entire course of human existence: we see it in the general evolution of the species as we ever adapt to changes in our natural environment; we see it in the development of civilization as we utilize our rational capacities to erect a secure foundation of science, technology, morality, law, and government to support and to improve our collective existence; we see it in the personal growth of each individual as he or she progresses through the human lifespan from birth to death. At the same time, we can also see that human existential success is contingent upon *adaptability* to change: the species *must* adapt successfully to the changes in its natural environment or it will become extinct; a civilization *must* adapt to the changes in its natural and cultural environment or it will decline or disappear altogether; an individual *must* adapt to the changes in his or her social environment as well as to the associated changes in the individual's way of thinking about his or her *integration* into that social environment, otherwise the individual will quickly become unhappy and fail to thrive. Our present discussion will focus upon the problems of ambivalence and self-deception which very often arise once a person has become aware of changes in his or her social environment, inasmuch as optimal personal growth is generally contingent upon one's early recognition and solution of such problems.

Let us consider the usual course of development of a typical individual. A person is conceived, sustained in the mother's womb for about nine months, born, and then raised from infancy by a supportive family which provides the wherewithal for the complete satisfaction of the person's needs, including such essentials and benefits as love, comfort, nourishment, cleanliness, shelter, protection, healthcare, socialization, education, acculteration, companionship, and entertainment. When the person passes from infancy to childhood, the sphere of personal education enlarges to include the services of a professional educator—

the teacher—to supplement and to improve upon the educational efforts of the parents, while the locus of personal education makes a gradual transition from the home to the school. When the person passes from childhood to early adolescence, the sphere of personal education continues to enlarge to include the services of a number of professional educators—teachers proficient in various areas of specialized knowledge—including such disciplines as language arts (to promote the further development of reading and writing skills in the language of the culture to which the person and the family of the person belong), foreign languages, mathematics, geography, history, and science. During this time, the person is gradually, and sometimes rather abruptly, becoming aware whether he or she, in general, is as intellectually competent as others, or more competent, or less competent, than others. The person is also becoming aware whether he or she has any inherent inclinations and singular abilities in particular fields of human accomplishment which distinguish him or her from others. By the time that the person passes from early adolescence to late adolescence and early adulthood, the education of the person has become more fully developed and specialized so that the person is finally prepared to choose and to enter a vocation, to earn a living, to make a useful contribution to the society of which the person is a member, and to provide the person with some sense of self-satisfaction and self-esteem. At this juncture in the person's life, it is often very unclear whether the person—by virtue of the personal achievements which have been attained and the personal choices which have been made—has acquired an excellent measure of self-understanding or if the person is simply as ambivalent as ever before with respect to himself or herself and his or her position within his or her social environment, albeit he or she may otherwise be in very close conformity with acceptable social norms. If the former alternative should indeed be the case, then the person will have crossed the threshold of personal authenticity so as to proceed in a new career with a feeling of contentment and a hope of attaining some small measure of personal success and happiness. On the other hand, if the latter alternative should be the case, then either the ambivalence which is felt by the person will subside with the passage of time as the person gradually identifies more closely with the career which has been chosen and pursued (and, as a consequence, the person at some point will cross the threshold of personal authenticity), or the ambivalence will gradually intensify, culminating in bad faith.

We need now to consider the causes and effects of bad faith when a young person embarks upon a new career. With respect to the *causes*, two possibilities come to mind. With the first, one begins a career, any career at all, because one *needs* to and one is *expected* to, even if one regrets giving up one's youthful dependence upon other people and, as a consequence, one is not yet emotionally prepared to pursue a personal career. With the second, one begins a *particular* career also because one is *expected* to—such as entering a family business with an aim to inherit it in the future, or beginning a career in a field that has been traditionally occupied by various ancestors of one's family in the past—even if one would much rather pursue an entirely different course. In either event, the young person is doing what he or she does not want to do; at the same time, the young person is not doing what he or she wants to do. The course of the process of either of these events generally comprises three phases. In the first, the young person is consciously unaware of the internalized conflict and he or she pretends to be fully committed to the career. In the second, he or she *does* become consciously aware of the conflict, either suddenly or gradually, but he or she continues to pretend to be fully committed. In the third, he or she gives up the pretence and begins to reveal substantial personal unhappiness resulting from the pursuit of the career. The obvious and inescapable *effects* of bad faith include existential contradiction, deceit, lost productivity, personal stagnancy, and increasing personal unhappiness.

Of course, to eliminate the detrimental consequences of any bad faith which may appear and persist in the thought and conduct of a young person once he or she first engages in a personal occupation, we should do whatever we can to eliminate the causes. The efforts must be accomplished long before the person becomes an adult, during the time of personal education, when the person is most amenable to the beneficial influences of other people. The efforts should encompass three broad objectives. The first: to teach a child to think for himself or herself as early as possible, because one who is early able to think for oneself is one who will most easily become able to act for oneself. The second: to provide a child with encouragements and opportunities to become self-reliant and self-sufficient, because one who possesses self-sufficiency and self-reliance will not impose an unfair burden upon others. The third: to allow a child to be free from unfair personal obligations to his or her parents, family, and teachers, because one who is free will most easily find one's own true path in life.

To continue our discussion, let us suppose that a young person has indeed previously acquired an excellent measure of self-understanding and self-confidence, with an absence of unnecessary and unjust demands from other people, so that he or she has been able to embark upon a new vocation with enthusiasm, happiness, and consequential success. Let us further suppose that some time has then passed, say, ten, twenty, or thirty years, since this early critical juncture in the person's life, since the time when the person passed from adolescence to adulthood, from dependence to independence, from inequality to equality. At this later point, the person may still be pursuing with undiminished enthusiasm, happiness, and success the occupation which had previously been chosen or else a new problem may gradually come to light. In this new situation, the person—having pursued the original occupation that had been chosen, and having had enjoyed it wholeheartedly at the beginning and perhaps for some while since—over time has become secretly unhappy with it, although outwardly still pretending to be fully committed to it. Giving rise to such a scenario are either of two different and unrelated reasons which underlie and go far to explain such a dramatic change of heart. We will now consider them in turn.

In one situation, the person has experienced a significant change of interests so that he or she has become dissatisfied with the original occupation. Perhaps that measure of self-understanding which one had initially attained has proven to become an exhausted, unsatisfactory, and considerably insufficient component within one's present magnitude of self-understanding. Perhaps one presently has a new grasp of, and an increasing interest in, certain areas of knowledge which, for that one, had previously been inaccessible and impenetrable. Perhaps one has become susceptible to the favorable influences of new people in one's life who have stimulated one to explore entirely new fields of human endeavor. Perhaps one has come to desire to provide assistance for one's spouse, or for another member of one's family, or for a close friend, but one is unable to do so in any adequate manner without giving up one's original occupation. We could easily continue to imagine any number of additional possible causes for the person's change of heart. The upshot of all of this, of course, is that the person is acting in bad faith: he or she is doing what he or she no longer wants to do, and he or she is not yet doing what he or she presently does want to do. The course of the process of acting in bad faith is here the same as that which we have previously described of the person who acts in bad faith upon, and subsequent to, the early critical juncture in that person's life. The effects of such bad faith are also the same. All efforts to eliminate the detrimental consequences of such bad faith may be much more difficult at this time, because one must rely upon oneself and upon those other persons close to oneself in one's life who may have sufficient awareness, concern, and ability to provide assistance to the person in improving the quality of his or her life.

In the other situation, the person remains committed to the occupation that he or she had chosen from the outset, but the occupation itself (or perhaps the entire industry of which it is a part) has declined in public value and is no longer useful, or some of the people with whom the person has been associated in a common effort to provide the products and services of the industry of which his or her occupation is a part (including perhaps even the superior to whom the person must report and upon whom the person and his or her work is ultimately dependent) have personally changed for the worse in one way or another over time and have fallen into disrepute. Then one may begin to question one's role in the performance, a performance which is generally no longer well received, even though one continues as always to play one's role to the best of one's abilities. Eventually, the person comes to act in bad faith: as in the previous situation which we have described, he or she is doing what he or she no longer wants to do, and he or she is not yet doing (perhaps because he or she has not yet even come to know) what he or she might otherwise like to do. The process is familiar: at first, the person is not consciously aware of his or her internalized conflict and he or she simply pretends to be fully committed to the occupation; then, the person *does* become consciously aware of the internalized conflict, but continues to pretend full commitment; finally, the person forsakes all attempts to continue to pretend and begins to reveal his or her unhappiness with the role which he or she has been obligated to play. The duration of this process of the exercise of bad faith may be brief or lengthy, but all courses of bad faith involve existential contradiction, deceit, lost productivity, personal stagnancy (often characterized by a sense of ennui, frustration, and hopelessness), and increasing personal unhappiness. In the end, all courses of bad faith are as detrimental to society at large as to all of such persons as may ultimately find themselves to have fallen into bad faith and to have become ensnared in its illusory cognitive-emotional trap. As in the earlier situation which we have described, all efforts to eliminate the detrimental consequences of bad faith during the middle and later stages of life may be much more difficult to accomplish than when a person enters early adulthood, because one's exposure to the beneficial influences of other people may be more limited, one's susceptiveness to such influences may be less pliable, and one's personal habits may be more rigid. Accordingly, the ultimate value and advisability of a well conceived, well executed, and highly effective program of education and wholesome personal development during late adolescence and early adulthood—a program which should encourage the relentless pursuit of self-understanding and the continuous cultivation of personal integrity—cannot be easily dismissed by any honest and wholly rational person.

3. INVOLVING INTERPERSONAL RELATIONSHIPS

The foregoing discussion has focused upon how the care and education of a person during the early years of life may best enable that person to avoid or to overcome illusory thinking and self-deception so that the person can quickly ascend to some minimal level (to penetrate a threshold, as it were) of self-awareness and personal authenticity in the course of choosing and pursuing an occupation. The course generally involves some network of interpersonal relationships of a varying degree of complexity such as is largely dependent upon the kind of work that has been chosen, but the focus most clearly has been trained upon the person and the person's choice and pursuit of a particular kind of work, not upon the interpersonal relationships, inasmuch as it is the person's interests and abilities such as have a more or less direct bearing upon the work which are essential, and not the interpersonal relationships, even in those instances where the interpersonal relationships are instrumental in the person's attaining a mastery of the work. We will turn now to consider the ill effects of illusory thinking and self-deception when a person enters into a course of interpersonal relationships with others *for its own sake* and not as a means to an end, as it most often is when one is choosing, learning, and pursuing an occupation. When a person enters into a course of interpersonal relationships with others for its own sake, a person is generally seeking a small number of persons—and quite often one particular person—with whom to develop and to sustain a close relationship in order to provide the person with some measure of reciprocity of communication, companionship, assistance, comfort, and pleasure throughout the future course of the person's life. Since one's control over one's situation is much more restricted when one is attempting to develop close interpersonal relationships than when one is pursuing an occupation, the ill effects of illusory thinking and self-deception are far more problematic and dangerous, are far less amenable to early detection and subsequent correction, and are far more likely to lead to self-surrender, to personal helplessness, and—at the very worst—sometimes even to self-destruction. All of this is so, of course, because a person has full, or almost full, control over his or her life when he or she is engaging in a personal occupation: if things are not working out too well, various adjustments can be made; if an improvement in performance is desired, better skills can be acquired or greater energy can be exerted. On the other hand, a person has only partial control over life when cultivating interpersonal relationships, because, by their very nature, human relationships between equals generally involve reciprocity. Each of the parties to the relationship has a portion—perhaps a half, perhaps a little or a lot greater or lesser than a half—of the control of the relationship: if both parties are dependable, the relationship will often work; if neither party is dependable, the relationship will usually not work; but if one is dependable while the other is not, then the one who is dependable will be hampered in his or her personal progress by the power of illusion and self-deception while the other, whether by deliberate intention or not, will be taking unfair advantage of the relationship.

Throughout the period of life extending from about midway in childhood, through adolescence, and into the early years of adulthood, a person is highly dependent upon relationships with peers—upon personal friendships, personal associations, and personal acquaintances—to enable the person to come to know his or her place in society, to discover his or her personal strengths and weaknesses in relation to those of others, and to develop a viable sense of self-awareness, self-possession, and personal authenticity. Several factors are involved in effecting the overall success of this process: the quality of one's intelligence, emotional well-being, and enthusiasm; the quality and richness of one's peer relationships; and the quality of one's society, education, and family relationships.

When things will have gone well, the person will have learned how to think for himself or herself; how to evaluate, and then to plan to improve, one's situation in the world; and how to regulate one's emotional responses to the endless vicissitudes of life. The person will have learned to see things as they are and to see other people for who they are; the person will have learned what things can be changed with ease and what things can be changed only with great difficulty, if they can be changed at all; likewise, the person will have learned, at least to some limited extent, whether one's influences upon others, or others' influences upon oneself, can effect change in oneself, or in others, with ease or only with great difficulty, if effecting change at all. Then we can say that the person has come to be able to see things truthfully; to act accordingly, effectively, and consistently; and, in consequence, is not very likely to waste his or her personal time, energy, and resources in continuous preoccupation with illusions.

When things will not have gone well, and the opposite of all of that which we have just discussed has become the case—because of one, or another, or some combination, of the factors which we have previously mentioned: poor family relationships, an inadequate education, a detrimental social environment, a low level of intelligence, low self-esteem, a low level of interest, a lack of enthusiasm, few opportunities to relate with one's peers, bad personal acquaintances, dangerous personal associations, unrewarding personal friendships—then the person will be all the more susceptible to illusionary thinking that can only yield the deleterious effects of false hope, instant gratification, and severe emotional volatility. Once this unhappy development has eventuated, it will be very difficult, and perhaps impossible, for one to improve one's present situation through one's own efforts, for the reason which we have previously cited, namely, that one inescapably (by virtue of the intrinsic nature of interpersonal relationships) loses much of one's direction and control over the future course of one's life once one has allowed oneself to become fully, or even partially, dependent upon another particular person, or upon certain other people. If one's level of intelligence is sufficiently high, it may be possible for one to learn from one's past experiences and to rectify the mistakes which one may have made over the course of that experience. Otherwise, one will always be highly dependent upon the personal discernment, concern, and advice of such older persons with whom one may have maintained close interpersonal relationships, or of any other persons of good quality with whom one may have formed attachments and may have subsequently developed similar close interpersonal relationships, for assisting him or her in overcoming illusionary thinking as it should come to determine in full, or even to influence in part, the choice and conduct of one's interpersonal relationships.

In summary, then, we can see that the power of illusion in personal affairs involving interpersonal relationships is even more harmful for human well-being—and even more difficult to avoid, to escape, or to overcome—than the power of illusion in personal affairs involving questionable beliefs and values, or in personal affairs involving work, and as a consequence, the ultimate value, desirability, and advisability of a well conceived, well executed, and highly effective program of education and wholesome personal development during late adolescence and early adulthood is all the more to be championed and advanced. Since human nature has greatly helped to identify, to describe, and to inform human beings throughout the long morning of the species, and since human nature has evolved but very slowly throughout that entire span of time, we should now be in an indisputable position to impart an unequivocal understanding of it to our young people through the course and progress of their upbringing and education, so that by the time that they are prepared to leave adolescence behind and to enter adulthood, all—or almost all of them—will not be misled by illusionary thinking, and consequently their adult lives will be all the more interesting, all the more rewarding, all the more enjoyable. Through—and *only* through—a steadfast faith in, and a constant exercise of, our human rational faculties, we can finally, decisively, and fully transcend the perennial regression in our cultural development, the unfathomable periodic failure of our common sense, and the intrinsically primitive baseness of our human nature.

BIBLIOGRAPHY

Aristotle. *The Nicomachean Ethics*. Trans. J.E.C. Weldon. Amherst, NY: Prometheus Books, 1987.

Bacon, F. *The New Organon*. 1620. Reprinted by Cambridge University Press, Cambridge, UK, 2000.

Barkow, J. H., Cosmides, L., and Tooby, J. (eds.) *The Adapted Mind*. New York, NY: Oxford University Press, 1992.

Confucius. *The Analects*. Trans. D. Hinton. Washington, DC: Counterpoint, 1988.

Darwin, C. *On the Origin of Species*. 1859. Reprinted by Cosimo, New York, NY, 2007.

Freud, S. *Moses and Monotheism*. Trans. K. Jones. New York, NY: Vintage Books, 1939.

Kierkegaard. S. *Either/Or*. 1843. Trans. A. Hannay. Abridged. Reprinted by Penguin Books, New York, NY, 1992.

MacLean, P. D. *The Triune Brain in Evolution: Role in Paleocerebral Functions*. New York, NY: Plenum, 1990.

Marx, K. *Capital*. 1867 (Vol. I), 1885 (Vol. II), 1894 (Vol. III). Reprinted by International Publishers, New York, NY, 1967.

Maslow, A. H. *Motivation and Personality*, 3rd Ed. New York, NY: Longman, 1987.

Mo Tzu. *Basic Writings*. Trans. B. Watson. New York: NY: Columbia University Press, 1963.

Sartre, J. *Being and Nothingness*. 1943. Trans. H. E. Barnes. Reprinted by Washington Square Press, New York, NY, 1992.

Taylor, C. T. *Moral Education in a Democracy*. Lanham, MD: University Press of America, 2012.

———. *Symbiosism*. Lanham, MD: Hamilton Books, 2006.

———. *Symbolism in Religion and Art*. Lanham, MD: University Press of America, 2008.

———. *Toward World Sovereignty*. Lanham, MD: University Press of America, 2002.

Tylor, E. B. *Primitive Culture*, 6th Ed. New York, NY; Putnam's Sons, 1920.

NAME INDEX

SUBJECT INDEX

www.ingramcontent.com/pod-product-compliance
Lightning Source LLC
Chambersburg PA
CBHW062044270326
41929CB00014B/2535